THE HAPPENING HAPPY HIPPY PARTY

ALEX HUNTER

For Sylvia

PROLOGUE

It was not good news for the Prime Minister.

In many ways, that did not make it 'news' as such. Most news, recently, had not been good for the Prime Minister. This information, however, merited snapping off the television and pouring another scotch with much clanging of glass.

"So," he said. "What now?"

Duncan Starling, the Downing Street director of communications, furrowed his brow. It was late. Almost all the Number Ten staff had gone home. The only eyes on them now belonged to the PM's predecessors, bearing down from their portraits. As the PM slurped his whisky, tie loose and sleeves rolled up, it was not clear whether they did so in sympathy or judgement.

"Well," began Starling. "You have several options, Prime Minister –"

"I don't want options," he barked. "I want a plan."

"We've come up with a number of possible responses that you can make about Alhabi –"

"I don't mean about *that*," he said, referring to another

explosion in the capital of the war-torn country that he had clumsily invaded.

"Oh?"

The Prime Minister walked to his desk and sat down in his big, leather chair. He drained the whisky.

"I mean about it all. Things are rough, Duncan. Very, very rough."

He wasn't wrong, thought Starling. Things had been rough for some time. As the security situation in Alhabi deteriorated, the situation at home was not much better either. The National Health Service was on the verge of meltdown, a status it shared with the immigration service, the police service, the fire service and the Home Office. In fact, the only part of the national infrastructure not reported to be on the verge of meltdown was the Driver and Vehicle Licencing Agency, but that might have been because the phone network and the Internet were on the verge of meltdown so it was difficult to know what was going on in Swansea.

Meanwhile, the parliamentary party circled around the Prime Minister like hungry sharks, the Opposition looked dangerously electable, and the far-right drew its life-force from the national discourse like a vampire.

"I agree," answered Starling, carefully.

The PM leaned back in his chair. "I know that the party has lots of clever ideas about how to win the general election, supported by lots of clever analysis. And that's good. That's great. But we need something more."

Starling pressed his palms together. "What do you have in mind?"

"What if we were to, shall we say, steer the enemy into a brick wall?"

"I don't follow."

He reached over to a decanter of water on his desk, and poured Starling a glass. "We need to insulate our electoral fortunes from our declining popularity."

"Go on."

"Do you remember Lord Flibbertigibbet Albatross-Saucepan?"

Starling blinked. "I – no, I've no idea who that is."

"Albatross-Saucepan stood as an independent for my seat in the last general election," he said, passing Starling the glass. "He was the one in the orange fish costume at the back of the stage."

"Oh, yes, I do remember," replied Starling, taking a sip of water. "Shouted 'justice for albatrosses' in the middle of the results. Lost his balance and fell off the stage."

"That's the chap. I think it must have been quite hard to see out of the fish costume. Real name Kevin Jones. I think he sells shower fittings."

Starling nodded. "What about him?"

The PM leaned forward. "He got quite a few votes you know, Duncan. Almost a thousand. For spending six weeks wandering around the constituency telling people his silly policies about social housing for stray dogs, custard for every school meal and reduced VAT on plumbing materials. People *liked* him."

"Liked him, of course. But they didn't elect him."

"But maybe enough of them would vote for him to destabilise the Opposition. Let's say we find some tiny, fringe party, every last one of them unelectable losers. A load of Albatross-Saucepans. Then we have them lifted into the public eye as an exciting new voice. The very *symbol* of an alternative government. We make sure that they launch a sensible manifesto, dominate the airwaves, eat into the actual Opposition – only for them to be torn apart by scandal at the last minute."

"But – why?"

The Prime Minister stood up and walked back to the whisky decanter. "Divide and conquer, Duncan. Their success will split the Opposition vote, and then their failure will create disillusion. Turnout will crash – and we'll be re-elected."

Starling stared at him. He wasn't sure what to say.

"It's certainly a novel idea, Prime Minister."

The PM poured another glass of scotch. "I want to announce a general election this week."

"But the plan does rather rely on finding a party so meat-headed that it doesn't realise what's happening," replied Starling. "And so mindlessly inept that it makes no political capital out of the adventure whatsoever. Where would you find such a party?"

L ondon. A cradle of democracy, a capital of global finance, and a cauldron of diplomacy. The city of Parliament, of Buckingham Palace, of Whitehall. The hub of an intellectual empire, an incubator of the brightest political discourse: The mother of a million epoch-defining ideas and the grandmother of ten million more. It was perfect place for the Happening Happy Hippy Party headquarters.

Except, of course, that the Happening Happy Hippy Party was not based in London at all, but in the small, coastal town of Sandport. A town so insignificant, in fact, that it only began appearing on the map in 1974 after someone at Ordnance Survey realised they had been mistaking it for a blemish on the lens of the aerial camera.

It was coming to the end of a typically grey Sandport day. A duvet of clouds rolled sleepily across the sky, seemingly satisfied that as long as the sun was kept out of sight then no further meteorological effort was necessary. Litter tumbled down the high street, the breeze depositing an empty fast food carton on the step of the Happening Happy Hippy Party headquarters.

HHHP Central had been purchased inexpensively at auction. It was a bargain, given its close proximity to the high street and its low council rates. This was chiefly because it was a disused public toilet, but upon renovation it was surprisingly comfortable, apart from the slight smell of ammonia. And that in the winter, jets of water would periodically shoot out of the wall where the urinals used to be.

On a Saturday six weeks before a general election, the HHHP was supposed to be out campaigning. It had dutifully – and somewhat miraculously – assembled at HHHP Central at nine in the morning for just that purpose. That was seven hours ago.

"I literally don't have enough fingers to count the reasons why burning the dead to generate electricity is a bad idea," said Catie, the director of communications. "There might not be enough *numbers* to count the reasons why burning the dead to generate electricity is a bad idea."

"Well, you raised no objection during the policy formulation stage," sniffed Rufus, the party's treasurer and the author of the manifesto.

"That's because I was *boycotting* the policy formulation stage! I was objecting to the entire manifesto! Each policy is sillier than the last!"

"That manifesto," growled Rufus, "is a tour-de-force of satirical irony. It's a masterpiece. It says, 'we won't conform to your patriarchal, neo-liberal political norms.' It says, 'we won't toe the line of the facile, vapid politics of yesteryear.'"

"What it says, Rufus, is '*we won't be elected.*'"

Dave Williams, the party leader, sighed. It had started with a two-hour debate about whether to canvass on the high street or the beach. That had proved to be a gateway into a much bigger row that had encompassed policy, strategy, socialism, post-truth society, feminism, public relations, globalism, East African coffee exports, something about lightbulbs and whether the moon landings really happened.

Leading the HHHP wasn't so much herding cats as herding wasps. Wasps that were on fire.

"Look," said Dave, "it's too late to change the manifesto, and we voted on it anyway," he added, catching Rufus's eye. "And I think if we really want to be elected, Catie, then perhaps we should actually put up a candidate for election."

"But then we would be participating in the bankrupt narrative of western social democracy!" said Rufus.

"As opposed to cleverly subverting it by sitting in an old public toilet on threadbare sofas?" replied Catie.

Dillon, the party secretary, stood up.

"I'm going to the pub."

That, agreed the whole HHHP – for the first time that day – was a good idea.

THE HIPPIES CUT an unusual but not unfamiliar figure as they shuffled out of the cold and into the comforting warmth of the blessed Duck and Fiddle. Their favoured table in the corner, tucked away next to a fruit machine that hadn't paid out in a decade, had seen a lot of debate over the years. It had been here that the party had been named. Here that Dave had been elected as leader. Here that Rufus had invented a device that used an inflatable toy and a length of plastic tubing to enable the consumption of a pint of beer in less than five seconds.

Catie led the way in a long, green trench-coat decorated with badges and patches for so many causes that she wasn't sure what some of them were anymore. She was followed by the looming figure of long-haired Dillon, looking like the grim reaper's recalcitrant, teenage son. Rufus, gaunt and tweed-jacketed, trailed behind.

Dave, who had to lock up HHHP Central, arrived a few minutes later. In a simple jumper and jeans, Dave had the least unusual appearance of the group – a fact that had assisted in his election to party leader. There was a mainstream tolerability to Dave Williams, a sort of steady normality that made him not so much appealing, as less unappealing than most of the available options.

Jack, the Duck's landlord, slammed his heavy palms on the bar. "So," he said. "What can I get you fine fellows?"

"Four pints of bitter, please, Jack," said Dillon, stooping to avoid the impressive seventeenth century beams that spanned the bar.

Dave watched Jack line up the pint glasses and haul the beer with an even hand. Jack was part of the Duck, as much as the ugly Toby jugs, old beer badges and uneven pool table.

"You fellows been out campaigning today, I suppose?" asked Jack.

"Um – today was a sort of policy formulation day," said Dillon.

"Well best of luck to you. Someone needs to kick that bugger Thorne into place. I heard someone in the post office saying that he'll be doing better than the Tories this time round. Nasty piece of work, he is."

"Well, we think so," replied Dillon.

"Better than the Tories?" said Dave. "Sorry, did you say Excelsior Thorne is expected to do better than the Tories?"

Jack shrugged, setting down the last of the beers. "That's what the bloke was saying in the post office. Article in the newspaper about it, he said. It's all about refugees, and immigrants, and Muslims, and the Russians."

Dave exchanged a glance of alarm with Dillon, and wordlessly raised his pint to his lips.

SOMEWHERE IN THE DARKNESS, Duncan Starling's phone was ringing. His hand bolted out from under the sheets and fumbled around on the bedside table, before seizing the handset and pulling it back under.

"Hello?" he said, without opening his eyes.

"Duncan! Good morning!"

"Hello, Prime Minister," murmured Starling, easing himself up on his elbows. He rubbed his eyes. '03:00' glared at him from the bedside in garish neon. His wife stirred, pulling more covers over her head.

"Duncan, I've got an update for you. We need to talk."

Starling cleared his throat. "Of course, Prime Minister – first thing in the morning?"

"It *is* first thing in the morning! I'm outside your house!"

Wearily, Starling clambered out of bed and felt for his bathrobe as the Prime Minister rapped on the front door. Mrs Starling mumbled something that sounded like a most uncharitable way to describe the Prime Minister of the United Kingdom of Great Britain and Northern Ireland.

Starling padded through his West London townhouse. The Prime Minister hardly slept. Four hours a night was his usual quota. It gave him an edge in politics, of course, but it made working for him difficult. It was worse when he was excited. He became a firewall of twenty-four hour energy when he was excited.

Starling unbolted and unlocked the door.

"Duncan!" beamed the Prime Minister. "I'm very excited!"

The Prime Minister and his entourage swept in like a gust of wind.

"Good morning, sir."

"It *is* a good morning! And good to see you in such fine form! Brush your hair."

Starling yawned. "It's three a.m., Prime Minister."

"Nonsense, it's at least ten past three. You don't want me to take off my shoes, do you now? No, of course not. Good, good. Come!"

The Prime Minister led Starling into his own kitchen. "I've found our targets!" he said, seizing Starling's kettle and shoving it under the tap. "Tea, boys?" he added, to his Special Branch protection officers.

"No thank you, sir," they both said in chorus.

"Good. Out you go, then."

They nodded and left the kitchen, closing the door and taking up positions in the hallway.

Starling sat down at the kitchen table, a hearty chunk of wood that his wife had fallen in love with after they had their first child. It was now the centre of the Starling household. "So – who?"

"This lot," answered the Prime Minister, slipping a dossier of photographs, a manifesto and biographical notes towards him.

Starling unfolded a pair of glasses and inspected the documents. "The Happening Happy Hippy Party," he murmured.

The Prime Minister slapped the kettle back down onto the worktop and flicked it on.

"Yep. Heard of them?"

"I don't think so."

"See? They're perfect. I hadn't either. Fresh, new, capture the imagination of the electorate and all that. They are, of course, complete jokers. Read the policies. Look at the one about climate change."

"We will off-set the dangerous changes to our climate by towing Britain two hundred miles north," read Starling aloud. "Where did you get this?"

"Never mind that, they're perfect. They're absolutely perfect."

Starling looked back down at the manifesto. "We will ease the burden on the NHS by making accidents illegal."

"Solid gold, isn't it?"

Starling fished in his bathrobe pocket, unsuccessfully, for some cigarettes. "Who is this guy, David Williams?"

"Their leader. A no-hoper. Held a few low-level jobs and then gave up work a few years ago to lead the party on a full-time basis. Seems to be on the dole now."

Starling opened an A4 envelope to reveal a couple of large, black and white photographs of Williams. They were taken from awkward angles, side-views, and one from behind a display of citrus-scented bleach.

He looked up. "These are surveillance photos, sir."

"Certainly are!" grinned the Prime Minister. "I had a very obliging firm of private investigators check them out."

Starling chewed his lip. "How big is this party?"

The Prime Minister was rummaging through Starling's cupboards, hunting for mugs. "They've had ups and downs. When they started, just a few, then peaked couple of years ago with a few hundred. They generated enough cash to buy a small building in some godforsaken town on the coast. That's more or less their only asset, and they've been on the wane ever since."

"Top cupboard, by the fridge, sir. But I thought you

wanted a party that would capture the public imagination?
That means they need to be viable. If re-nationalising the
railways is loony enough in this political climate, then advo-
cating moving the entire country is absurd. Nobody will
take it seriously. They'll think it's a joke. It *is* a joke."

The Prime Minister retrieved two mugs, set them on the
worktop, and smiled his wide, election-winning smile.
"With money, and a few pokes in the right direction, it won't
be long before they revise their stance. We can't use a party
with marbles, Duncan – if they have too much sense they'll
capitalise on their moment in the public eye. We need the
last clowns in the circus – a shower of idiocy, hardwired to
short-circuit. So we give them a manifesto and the funds,
massage their way into the festering sore of the public's
consciousness, and let them do what they do best. Cock up.
Well, with a bit of encouragement."

"It does sound pretty far-fetched sir, not to say risky –
very risky."

The kettle clicked off as a column of billowing steam
coiled up towards the ceiling.

The Prime Minister smiled his wide smile again. "Mine's
tea, milk, two sugars. Thanks, Duncan."

A FEW HOURS after Duncan Starling was rudely awoken by
the Prime Minister, Dave Williams was standing in his bathroom, and staring into the mirror.

Dave's reflection stared back as he shaved. It wasn't a
handsome reflection, but it wasn't an ugly one either. Most
things about Dave were decidedly average – five foot eight,
brown hair, blue eyes, a veteran of the typical route of the
middle-class twenty-something: University, at which he had

met Dillon, followed by uninspiring employment. Or, in Dave's case, uninspiring un-employment punctuated by short bursts of inconvenient but paid activity.

He tapped the foam out of the razor, tightened the towel around his middle, and started on the other side of his face.

Dillon had not exactly set the world alight since graduating either, having spent his post-university days working in a little bookshop in town. He, at least, seemed to have a lower threshold for success than Dave. They let him go to work barefoot, which seemed to be the most important thing to him. Dave had been more restless. He had wanted to *do something*. Change something. That was the drive that had led to the establishment of the HHHP. That was four years ago.

Dave rinsed his face, stopping briefly as he caught sight of his belly, hanging inquisitively over the edge of his towel. He prodded it. That wasn't there last month, surely?

He shuffled out of the bathroom and to the kitchen, pausing at the front door to pick up the newspaper. *Doing something* had turned out to be rather more complicated than he had thought. Whether it was due to the 'patriarchal colossus' to which Catie referred, or the 'neo-liberal machine' that Rufus despised, Dave wasn't sure. A 'patriarchal colossus' rather sounded like something that might emerge from a spaceship and chase him down the street, while he wouldn't recognise a 'neo-liberal machine' if it started beeping at him angrily and squawking about too many items in the bagging area. What he did know, however, was that it was bloody difficult to get anything significant done in Sandport, never mind Britain.

He looked down at the paper, the cover slightly blackened where Ken, his flatmate, had trodden on it on his way out.

DAVE STUMBLED into the Duck and Fiddle, nearly spilling the pint of an elderly gentleman dawdling near the entrance. He spotted Ken immediately, quietly nursing a beer and watching a football game on TV. Dave strode over, stood directly in front of him and slammed the newspaper down the table.

"What?" said Ken, straining to see the TV around Dave's head.

"Look at it!"

Ken briefly glanced at the paper, and then returned his gaze to the TV. "So I forgot to pick it up off the floor today, sorry."

"No, the headline – the headline!"

Ken sighed, and reluctantly looked at the cover. "Massingbird. The MP. Heart attack. Very sad. Fine."

"Do you know what this means?

"That he, at least, isn't going to be blocking my view of the TV?"

Dave sat down and took a slug of Ken's pint. "It means that for the first time in twenty-five years, Massingbird's majority is up for grabs! It means *this seat* is going to be vacant in the general election!"

"I wish that seat was vacant now," growled Ken.

"This could be it, Ken."

Ken stared at Dave for a moment, then sighed again and gave up on the TV.

"Look, Dave," he said. "You need to let this go. It's not healthy. You've got no supporters, no job – you hardly ever pay rent. I only let you live with me because you hang around the house all day and I don't trust next door not to nick my laptop while I'm at work. And look," he added, pointing out of the window to the bakery across the road, where a bright red poster emblazoned with a black 'BF' hung proudly in the window. "It's not like the competition isn't stiff. BEEF think this could be their first parliamentary seat. It's scary."

The British English Emancipation Front. Dave shuddered at the sight. "Well maybe the time has come to take them on. The great battle for the heart of the British people, between two titanic opposed forces! One of oppression, and one of hope!"

"Titanic forces? Dave, you nearly called yourselves the Smiley Happy Anarchist Group."

"I liked that. It had a joyous ring to it."

"The acronym was 'SHAG'."

"I don't follow."

Ken took a mouthful of beer. "Dave, mate, this is a fantasy. You're playing. This holds you back. You're, what, thirty-something now? This should be a hobby, not your life. Don't you want to achieve something?"

Dave swallowed. He'd quite like a beer himself. But there was, as always, a cashflow issue.

"You see that poster out there?" Ken went on. "That vomit-splash of fascism stuck to that window by a local businesswoman who probably watches cooking shows and is kind to her cats? You know what that is? That's the result of years of alienation. That's terror sown by endless hour news of horrors worldwide. That's her shrinking profits while huge, faceless corporations suck up her customers with gutter-low prices she could never afford to charge. That's her rage as every politician gives her half-answers, no-answers and fake answers."

"Well – "

"That's her crying for reassurance, and clinging to the

first lifeboat that comes along. She doesn't care if the lifeboat's playing Wagner and everybody's wearing a smart, black uniform. That's what's real here, Dave. Do you really think your teenage clubhouse can take that on?"

Dave paused. He imagined her in the voting booth, putting her cross next to Excelsior Thorne's name. "Maybe I do," he said. "Maybe we can. Maybe if people want authenticity then that's what we offer. We're real."

"Yeah, you do have that. You definitely get what you pay for with you guys. But not in a reassuringly-expensive way. More in a what-happens-if-you-eat-sushi-two-hundred-miles-inland, out-of a-dumpster, kind of way."

"You're not a believer, Ken. I can see that. But I think we can change this. I wonder what the others are doing?"

"Watching the game, probably," said Ken, bitterly.

THE PRIME MINISTER'S JAGUAR swept through the black, iron gates of Downing Street and out into London, flanked by police motorcyclists and followed by an unmarked police car.

Duncan Starling sat in the back with the Prime Minister and Amy Cordell, one of Starling's senior staff. Slightly bleary-eyed, Starling had been making notes on his smartphone ahead of their appointment across the river. Amy was glaring moodily out of the window.

"So," he said, slipping the phone into his pocket and turning to the Prime Minister. "How exactly are you going to inject sufficient funds and expertise into the HHHP to propel them to such dizzying heights?"

The Prime Minister was admiring the twinkling blue

lights of the police motorcycles. Starling knew the PM got a kick out of that. He knew he'd miss it if they lost.

"Hm? Oh yes, them – I have a two-stroke strategy."

"Go on."

The Prime Minister turned his gaze back into the car. "They're about to receive an extremely generous donation to the party from a very wealthy admirer, and a membership application from an impressive, dynamic political expert who will steer them in the right direction."

Starling nodded, but didn't for a moment think it would be that easy. He had begun composing the usual mental list of concerns. This one would be long, though. Longer than the time the Prime Minister wanted to interfere in the political unrest of a South American country, because he feared a revolution would upset his holiday plans. Longer even than the time he wanted to use the SAS to resolve a dispute over a malfunctioning iPod he bought on Ebay.

"Who is the admirer?"

"That, Duncan, is who we're off to meet this afternoon! Well, I say 'meet.' I mean see. Of sorts. We'll go on the way to this grotty hospital."

"It's a hospice actually, sir."

The Prime Minister's eyes narrowed. "Cancer people?"

"That's – that's right."

Starling watched him nod in silence. He knew what the man was doing. Nine years in government together told him that. The PM was deciding which face to use for the visit. Would it 'deep concern,' 'quiet indignation,' or 'steely resolution'? There was an election afoot, after all.

"Sir, where's the money going to come from? Election campaigns cost millions. Who would pay for it, just to save y– the government?"

"Don't you worry about that," smiled the Prime Minister

with the wide, paternalistic grin often used by politicians to convey mastery. "All will be explained."

"That money will be traceable, you know."

"Relax, Duncan! It's all going to be fine. You'll work your usual magic, ensure that nobody in Fleet Street looks too closely."

Starling filed that for later. "And the new member? Who's that going to be?"

"Easy," replied the Prime Minister. "It's Amy."

Starling glanced across at Amy, who stared back, her face more thunderous than any rainstorm Starling had encountered in his lifetime.

"Oh. Well, congratulations, Amy."

"Thanks," she said, acidly.

"Now," went on the Prime Minister, opening a briefing folder on his lap and flicking through the loose sheets inside. "Shall I use the speech where we promise a hundred mil to cancer research, or a hundred mil to cancer patients?"

A BELL TINKLED as Dave opened the door and walked into the bookshop. It was deserted, and he weaved his way between the displays to the counter at the back.

And then he stopped. One display was topped with a sign reading 'LOCAL AUTHOR!' and featured a big photograph of Excelsior Thorne, the leader of the British English Emancipation Front. It was atop a crisp, freshly-printed stack of books entitled 'Keep Right: The Right to be Right and All Right, Right? Right!'

Dave frowned.

"May I help you?" asked a disembodied voice.

Dave turned to find that the shopkeeper had appeared

behind him. He turned back to gesture at the display. "Are you really selling this book?"

"Oh yes, of course. They're selling very well," said the shopkeeper, straightening the books.

"Really? Excelsior Thorne's book?"

"Of course. Mr. Thorne is a well-respected pillar of the community. A most erudite gentleman."

"You're kidding, right? This – this is a racist book. He's a fascist."

"Oh no, young man, oh no, not at all. He's hot-tipped to win this seat in the general election. He's a no-nonsense, shoot-straight-from-the-hip sort of fellow. A straight-talker, you see. I think it makes for a very readable book."

There was a short pause. Dave couldn't think of anything to say.

"Is there anything particular you require, young man?"

"Is Dillon working today?"

"Other counter, back of the shop."

Dave nodded, and wordlessly left the shopkeeper. He saw Dillon's enormous bare feet propped up on the counter before he encountered the man himself, a huge tropical shirt flowing around him. Dillon was fast asleep, an open packet of sweets next to him.

Dave tapped a little bell-button to summon Dillon's attention, but he failed to stir. Dave hit the bell again, and again, but without success. He sighed, and put his hand into the bag for a sweet. It rustled.

Dillon opened one eye. "Hey! Oh, Dave!" He sat up.

"Hey Dillon, how's it going?"

Dillon shrugged. "Not much going on today."

"So I see. Not much sign of you rejecting the nefarious machinery of capitalism then?"

"Well, way I see it, supporting local business helps fight

back against the colonial might of massive online book-sellers. And it pays the bills. It's not so bad. They let me expand my mind in the stockroom whenever I want."

"Seriously?" said Dave in a hushed voice. "Weed? Here?"

"Oh no," replied Dillon. "I meant, like, Shakespeare and stuff."

"Oh – yes."

"So, what's up?"

"You heard the news?"

Dillon shrugged. "About?"

"Peter Massingbird?"

"Nope."

"He's dead. Died at the weekend. Which means that this constituency's going to be - "

"Vacant," nodded Dillon.

Dave perched himself on the counter and helped himself to sweets. "Yep. Sandport's not going to be a safe Tory seat at the election without Massingbird. We're in with a chance."

"Ah," said Dillon, biting his lip. "So, you're thinking of – fighting the seat?"

Dave stared at Dillon. "Yes, of course, yes!"

Dillon sighed. "Dave, we say we're 'in with a chance' every time. Last general election, the local council elections – and we never win."

"You mean you're thinking of not even contesting the election?"

"Well, no," admitted Dillon with a shrug. "I mean, it's fun and all, but are we really cut out for politics, Dave? Face it, we're playing at this. Thorne might be evil, but he's professional."

Dave glanced back through the shop towards the display

of Thorne's book. A middle-aged lady in a nurse's uniform was thumbing through a copy.

"We can change this year, Dillon," said Dave, turning back to him. "With your help. We'll grow the party, we'll publish a manifesto, invest in a campaign, remember to vote. Sandport won't know what's hit it!"

"Sandport not knowing what hit it was always the problem. Because we never really hit it. We just sort of brushed lightly past it in the corridor."

"You can't tell me that sleeping in a bookshop all afternoon is what you were put on this planet to do, Dillon."

"Oh, come on, Dave – like your life's purpose is to lie around Ken's flat all day, watching daytime TV shows where angry northerners argue about whose dog got whose pregnant? How would we fund a campaign? You haven't even got a job."

Dave frowned.

"I'm sorry," said Dillon. "I didn't mean it like that."

"Let's at least give it one last shot, Dillon."

"Okay, okay," conceded Dillon, raising his hands in the air. "Let's say we did decide to give it a go. But the point about funds stands. There's nothing. No money, no assets apart from HHHP Central, a campervan and five thousand leaflets with 'happening' spelled wrong. There can be no campaign without funds. And we've got no funds."

Dave sighed. Dillon had a good point.

He had a *really* good point.

THE LOW GROWL of London seemed to maintain a respectful distance at the walls of the cemetery, leaving the tombstones and flowers standing silently in the birdsong. It was a bright, cloudless morning, and the cemetery was empty apart from a small group at one particular grave.

Starling found these places oddly soothing. Maybe that was because he had spent so much time in one of them as a boy. He would save his pocket money, buy flowers at a small shop on the corner and sit at the feet of his mother. He would chat to her for hours.

He glanced back at the entrance, looking away from his memory as much as the scene before him. Outside the gate, two Jaguars purred obediently. Two plain-clothed Special Branch officers hovered nearby. Another stood a little distance away amidst the tombstones, another under a tree behind them.

Thick clouds of steam curled out of Starlings mouth as he spoke. "So, sir – where is the donor?"

The two men stood in long, grey overcoats. Starling's hands were dug deep into his pockets.

"You're looking at him," murmured the Prime Minister.

Starling looked down. The grave was freshly covered, a new marble headstone sparkling in the sun. A single bouquet of flowers sat on the mound of earth, crispy in the morning frost.

"The – the grave?"

The Prime Minister nodded.

"Who is it?"

"Does it matter?" shrugged the PM. "Don't know, really."

There was a pause.

"Probably better that way," he added.

"But who – how?" Starling whispered. "*MI5*?"

"Gracious, no. Couple of chaps in the City actually, went to university with them. Great pals, splendid fellows. Could mine-sweep with the best of them. Anyway, yes, they owe me a favour or two. They made the necessary arrangements."

"You mean they – " Starling glanced at the Special Branch officers and lowered his voice further. "Knocked him off?"

"Good lord, no! No, this chap died naturally. *Opportunity*, Duncan. It's all about opportunity."

Starling digested this. "So, this guy's money is going to the party – sir, this is illegal. It's theft."

The Prime Minister shook his head. "Not *his* money, no. This chap died without a penny to his name. Very sad. No, that money will be funnelled through his will. Very simple, very clean. Whatever this loser was in life, he'll be a bloody hippy in death."

Starling reached into his breast-pocket and drew out a packet of cigarettes. He was meant to be cutting down. All that meant in a job like this was that he bought half-size packs, twice as often. He flicked one out, lit it with a zippo and inhaled sharply.

"How much money?" he asked finally, exhaling.

"Ten million pounds."

"What?" exploded Starling, unable to contain himself. The cigarette fell out of his mouth, twirling down to the flowers.

The Prime Minister's brow furrowed. "Duncan, please. Contain yourself."

"Where the hell did that much money come from?"

"Well, it seems there are a couple of West African businessmen who are very keen to impress me. There's a war going on over there, you know. Terrible business. They want some good, sturdy British weapons to sort that mess out. Machine-guns that don't jam. Grenades that don't go off at the wrong moment. Fine British products. It will be an honour to help arrange mutually-beneficial contracts between our stalwart industries and these fine customers."

Starling rubbed his face in nervous alarm. This wasn't good. None of this was good. "Prime Minister, this is very, very irregular. One whiff of this to the press, just one whiff –"

"Duncan, relax," he replied, an edge of irritation entering his voice. "My chums have been most efficient. It's amazing what international co-operation can do. The money has filtered through several West African bank accounts and a couple of companies whose names suggest that they have something to do with bananas. It ultimately lands in a bank account in Kundunga, West Africa, before being moved to an account in the name of this fellow." The Prime Minister smiled, darkly. "And this is my favourite bit – the Kundungan account is in the name of a Mr David Williams."

Starling's eyes widened. "The money has already been linked to the HHHP?"

The Prime Minister stepped forward, extinguishing the dying cigarette on the grass under his expensive shoe. "If someone does look into it – *when* someone looks into it – it's all going to come back to the HHHP."

Starling opened his mouth to say something, but no words came out. Shady dealings were a part of government. But leaking misinformation to the press was one thing. Sinister, illegal arrangements with corrupt West African regimes was quite another.

The Prime Minister seemed to take Starling's silence as a compliment. "Ingenious, yes? I think a couple of people will be needing a mention in the Queen's Birthday Honours, don't you?"

With that, the Prime Minister flicked a single pound coin onto the grave, and strode towards the cars.

"C-Cash for honours," blurted Starling. "There'll be a scandal!"

"Scandal?" Laughed the Prime Minister, turning back. "How? The money's going the *other* way! Come on Starling, we'll be late for this hospital. Hospice. Cancer people. Whatever."

He made to turn again to walk away, but then stopped, and said: "If we stay here any longer, they'll end up visiting *us!*"

He laughed again through the broad smile for which he was so famous. Eleven years in power had weathered his face and haggard his features, but the smile was as brilliant as it had ever been. Starling knew it well. It was the only part of his face that didn't require airbrushing on the cover of the party manifesto.

Starling rammed his hand back into his breast-pocket and seized the cigarette packet.

"Mr. Williams, one must confess one's sincere pleasure at your landslide victory. We hoped, so deeply, that your party would command a majority in the house and it is my delight – no, my honour – to invite you to form a government."

Dave strolled through the immaculate gardens of Buckingham Palace, at the side of Her Majesty the Queen.

"Your Majesty I assure you – the honour is all mine," he replied.

They stopped, as did the two corgis padding obediently at their feet. The Queen turned to Dave, and held his gaze.

"Mr. Williams, I find that, now I have met you, you

exude an authority and a charm that I have not encountered in a Prime Minister since dear, dear Harold."

There was a pause. She leaned in and, in almost a whisper, added, "I trust you implicitly."

"Thank you, your Majesty," said Dave.

"Dave, have you seen any clean socks?" said Ken.

"What?"

"I had some drying on the radiator next to that kebab which, it turns out, has also vanished."

"What the hell are you doing at Buckingham Palace?"

"At *where*?"

Dave opened his eyes through a fog of headache, morning breath and dehydration. The elegant gardens were gone, replaced by his dirty little flat and his dirty little flatmate.

"Oh," he groaned, rubbing his temples.

Ken looked at him for a moment, sprawled on the sofa surrounded by beer cans and what appeared to be a kebab wrapper. "Queenie again?"

Dave nodded.

Ken's thin, underpants-clad frame weaved gingerly between empty pizza boxes and video game sleeves. He began dismantling the sofa as he continued his sock investigation. "You need to stop the Queen dreams, bro. It's not healthy. And you also need to stop nicking my socks and eating my kebabs."

Satisfied that the sofa was sock-free, Ken tottered away to continue his search elsewhere.

"Oh," he said, turning back and throwing an envelope over to Dave. "And you've got post."

Dave inspected the envelope with suspicion. Unlike most of his post, it did not have anything stamped in red on the front. He tore it open, to find a letter written on good-quality paper. This in itself was intriguing, as Dave didn't know anybody that wrote on good-quality paper. At least not when they wrote to him. He sniffed it, then unfolded it, and began to read.

Bang bang bang!
  Bang bang BANG!
  Bang BANG bang!

"All right, all right, I'm coming, I'm coming," shouted Jack as he shuffled across the Duck and Fiddle as fast as his dressing gown and slippers would allow him. He fumbled in his pocket for the keys, and slid back the bolts.

  BANG bang bang!
  BANG BANG BANG!

"All right!" he shouted, finally locating the correct pair of keys and unlocking the door. He pulled it open, blinking as the cold, bright morning settled on his face.

"Jack," said a voice, its owner pushing past him in a blur that looked rather a lot like Dave Williams.

"What the hell? Dave, it's nine in the morning!"

Dave was suddenly behind the bar, grabbing a pint glass of questionable cleanliness and filling it with beer. "Need a drink," he said.

"I thought it was an emergency – maybe the police or something," growled Jack.

"It *is* an emergency," breathed Dave, before raising the pint of beer to his lips and downing the entire glass in three huge gulps. He slammed the glass down on the bar with a loud burp, and paused for a moment, assessing the effects.

"Another," he concluded, and shoved the glass back under the tap.

As the second beer disappeared into Dave, Jack closed the door, re-set the locks, and reached up to one of the wooden beams where he kept a baseball bat. It had been inexplicably left in the bar one evening, and had proven occasionally useful.

Dave's eyes didn't flinch over the glass. With his other hand, he produced a crumpled piece of paper from a pocket and tossed it over to Jack.

Jack rested the baseball bat on a table and fished around in his pocket for his spectacles, unfolded them, and began to read.

'*Dear Mr Williams,*

'*I trust this letter finds you well. I have been instructed by Plumpton Bradley, the executors of the estate of Mr Winstanley Mortimer, that a considerable sum is to be bequeathed to the Happening Happy Hippy Party by the late Mr. Mortimer.*

'*I am therefore contacting you in your capacity as a representative of the Happening Happy Hippy Party to begin the process of transferring these funds to you. Please contact my practice at your earliest convenience to discuss these proceedings.*

'*Yours sincerely,*

Harold Fisk.'

Dave's pint glass, now empty again, hit the bar. Jack glanced at Dave's wide eyes, joined him behind the bar and fished out a wad of stapled paper from a Toby jug.

"Am I to presume then," he murmured, "that you'll be paying your tab?"

"DID DAVE SAY WHAT HE WANTED?" asked Dillon, as he and Rufus trudged towards the Duck and Fiddle. Their pace was brisk, and Dillon's long, black overcoat served him better in the chill of the morning than his frilly poet blouse. It had not been long before Rufus had complained that his own choice of colourful tropical shirt and baggy, cotton trousers may have been ill-considered.

"Nope," replied Rufus. "Just said to come to the Duck. Sounded pretty excited though. I think he might be drunk."

Dillon sighed. "At nine-thirty in the morning. Well, that's a development. How did you know?"

"Because he called it the 'Fuckandiddle'."

Rufus opened the door and the two entered the pub, glad of the warmth inside.

Dillon took a moment to examine the scene before them. He noted two potentially pertinent features. The first was that Jack was standing at the bar in his dressing gown, carefully examining what appeared to be a cheque. The second was that Dave was sitting at a table on his own, accompanied by five empty pint pots, an ashtray and a cigar. A bottle of inexpensive white wine was sitting in a bucket surrounded by bags of frozen peas. He was sprawled across his chair, grinning widely.

"Hooray!" he cheered, opening his arms to welcome them.

"Er, good morning, Dave," said Dillon. "What's going on? What's with the wine and peas?"

"He wanted chilled champagne on ice," said Jack with a sigh. "That was the best I could do."

Dillon and Rufus pulled a pair of chairs over and sat down. Dave thrust a piece of paper at them.

"Read it and weep," he slurred.

With a glance at Rufus, Dillon inspected the sheet carefully.

"Dave," he said. "This is a bar menu."

"Oh, yeah, hang on," Dave rummaged around, eventually found Harold Fisk's letter, and waved it in Dillon's direction instead. "Barkeep," he called out. "Two more of your finest gentlemens for these pints of ale!"

Jack glared at Dave. The baseball bat had not yet returned to its beam.

Dillon read the letter, then flipped it over to look at the reverse, and handed it to Rufus.

"It's a wind-up, Dave."

Dave shook his head. "No, no, no. Harry Fisk and me go way, way, back. Way back. All the way back. Back beyond the way. He wouldn't do that. He's a good lad. He went to Cambridge, you know."

"Cheers Jack," said Dillon, as two more beers appeared on the table. "Yeah, but Dave, Harold Fisk didn't necessarily send it. Anyone can write in his name and send it to you."

Dave leaned forward, scowling. "Are you calling Harry Fisk a liar?"

"Well – well no, just someone writing in his, er, name."

"But it's his signature!"

"How do you know?"

"'Cos he's my solicitor, innhe? He's written me, like, tons of times." Dave waved the cigar around in the air to emphasise his point. It did not lend him the gravitas he imagined, not least as it had gone out. "He went to Cambridge, you know," he added.

Dillon sipped his pint. "Call him then. See if it's true."

"I can't."

"Why?"

"'Cos I dropped my phone in my beer by mistake and now the screen doesn't work."

Rufus had finished reading. "Use mine," he said, reaching into his pocket. "Actually, maybe I should do it on your behalf."

Dave shrugged. "Yeah, probably. I think I might not sound professionalable."

Rufus tapped in the number, and held the phone to his ear.

WHEN CATIE ARRIVED at the Duck at around ten thirty, she found Dave, Rufus and Dillon sitting around three buckets of frozen peas and cheap white wine.

"Hello boys," she said, warily.

"Hooray!" They cheered, opening their arms to welcome them.

"It's pretty early for a party."

"Check it out!" grinned Rufus from behind a cigar, handing her the solicitor's letter. Catie took it and read it as she sat down.

"What does this mean? We've been left some money?"

Dave giggled like a child. "Some money," he repeated. "How much, tell her how much Dilly-o!"

"Only if you promise never to call me 'Dilly-o' again, Dave."

"Well, come on then," said Catie. "How much?"

Dillon cleared his throat. "Ten million pounds."

Catie laughed. "Yeah, all right. Very funny."

"No, it's true," said Dillon. "We phoned the solicitor. It's completely legit. Dave and I are going to see him tomorrow."

"Whatever," replied Catie. "So, are we actually going to do some work on the blog today?"

Dave and Dillon exchanged glances. "Catie – we won't have just a blog anymore, we'll have a bloody *newspaper*."

Rufus stabbed the air with his cigar. "*Hippy Times*! I like it."

Catie sat down. "Guys, come on. We need to do some work."

Dillon shrugged. "How can we convince you of this?"

"Oh, Dillon," she sighed. "I'm not biting. And this joke's getting old quickly."

"Or *Hippy News*. No wait – *The Happening*!" said Rufus.

Catie shot him a dangerous glance.

"*Times* it is," he said, raising his hands.

"I'm saying its genuine," said Dillon. "You know you can trust me."

Catie shook her head. "Sorry, Dillon. No sale."

"We could phone the solishitor again," suggested Dave.

"Yeah, and he'd be in your little game, wouldn't he?"

"Well, then I just don't know what we need to say to you, Catie," sighed Dillon.

"Young lady," said the gruff voice of Jack, appearing at Catie's side. He placed one of his big, warm hands on her shoulder and showed her the cheque. "If it helps," he went on, "Dave has paid his tab."

Catie stared at him, and then at the cheque.

"Holy tits, we're rich," she said.

2

T he HHHP was not the only party skating around the fringes of British politics. Britain's vibrant political culture had a proud history of electoral runner-ups. Ever-hopeful stalwarts lined the back of the stage on election night, their stoic faces obscured by the yellow, red or blue rosettes at the front. They were the ones who trod the streets, peddling leaflets and talking feverishly about the closure of a hospital or the incompetence of the council. They faced the wind and rain with little more than their steely gaze and withered rosettes, wrestling as much with the weather as the ambivalence of passers-by. Most of them were just trying to make the world a better place. Most of them.

Then there was the British English Emancipation Front.

Martha Lewandowski, the political editor of the *Sandport Chronicle*, sat in an upscale café with BEEF's leader, Excelsior Thorne. Thorne didn't need to know that being the 'political editor' at Sandport's biggest-selling local newspaper also meant being the entire political department.

Neither did he need to know that 'biggest-selling' was best considered a highly caveated, relative description.

Martha's coffee sat mostly untouched, as Thorne talked about his party's rising popularity and she scrawled in her notebook. Thorne sipped water.

"You see," he was saying. "I think the problem that many of our people had in the past, was how they expressed their frustrations. They allowed themselves to become a kind of caricature, rather than express their legitimate concerns in ways that resonated. And that's what we do now. That's why we're capturing the imagination of the people, Martha."

This was not an interview Martha particularly wanted to do. Giving a platform to a party that had advocated some very grim things was not in keeping with her values. But BEEF's popularity forced her hand – mainly through the vessel of her editor, who pointed to local opinion polls showing BEEF's growing lead. That needed to be addressed. Reluctantly, she had to agree.

"You don't think it has more to do with the army of professional consultants you guys brought in to make-over your image?" she said.

Thorne smiled.

BEEF, and its unwieldy name, were the products of faction mergers in Britain's far-right in the nineties. Thorne's ascension to power had been meteoric and unforeseen – aided in no small way by a freak bus crash in which the other leadership contenders had been wiped out. An investigation led to a trial, which had, of course, acquitted Thorne of any involvement in that horrible, random tragedy.

After that traumatic setback for BEEF, it had been success after success, with new members joining daily. Good luck seemed to befall BEEF and everyone connected with it.

That even included those only loosely linked to the party; such as the judge who had presided over Thorne's trial and most of the jury. They had won large sums in the Cambodia State Lottery, which was particularly fortunate as none of them had ever been to Cambodia and were the first-ever winners of the lottery – which, apparently, went bankrupt immediately after the pay-out and folded.

And so, Excelsior R. Thorne, a man who haggled with *Big Issue* vendors, became the leader of one of the UK's most prominent right-wing movements. And he was perfectly on time. The country had never been more divided. Ethnic tensions, rising xenophobia, gaping economic inequality, widespread political disenfranchisement and the polarising effect of social media all played into his hands.

It was a good time to be Excelsior Thorne.

"Hey, I'm no schmoozey politico, Martha. I'm a self-made man. I made my own successes. You know, when I went out into world, I had just one thing – a big dream."

Martha looked up. "Well, yes, that – and three million pounds from your father."

"A little seed money, sure – but who doesn't?"

"You invested the money in a string of companies, then, right? Mostly, shall we say, not-at-all to moderately successful?"

Thorne chuckled. "That's not true. They were some great companies, we had happy customers and clients all over the place."

"The first one was a lobbying firm – Thorne In The Side Limited."

"Well – political consultancy, yes."

"You worked for big tobacco, big pharma, extractives, global finance – some of your clients were not very popular people."

"Martha, you know, it's all part of the rich political tapestry of democracy."

"That was until jellygate, of course."

Thorne shook his head. "Those allegations were totally unfounded. We had nothing to do with that."

"Big paddling pool filled with jelly, two mostly-naked MPs from a committee on tobacco regulation, six ladies even more naked than the MPs, all rolling around having a wonderful, wibbly-wobbly time? You know, until the police came. Rather earlier than anyone else involved, I imagine."

"The left-wing media were very unfair."

"But Thorne In The Side Limited folded straight after those MPs resigned, right?"

"Look, that's a lot of jelly under the brid – I mean, water under the bridge."

"So, you moved quickly on to your next project. You made collars for pets – cats and dogs. Nigel Pawthorne Collars Limited, yes?"

Thorne took a sip of water and put the glass down. "That litigation was very unfair."

"But the materials you used weren't safe, right? Cheap, but unsafe?"

"They were perfectly safe! Those cats went bald from natural circumstances!"

"All of them?"

"Nothing was ever proven," snapped Thorne. "And I don't know why people complained, either. Bald cats are more convenient. Who wants cat hair all over their house?"

"I think that might have been the problem, Mr Thorne – people generally prefer it on their cats."

"Look," said Thorne. "We settled out of court because we wanted to move on to other things, not because we accepted any responsibility."

"Okay," replied Martha. She put her pen down and looked up. "But your clothing brand was more successful, wasn't it? ThorneChic. You passed an ethical audit – no child labour in your Asian factories, just some really positive social outreach projects employing disabled people."

"Absolutely, Martha. Those Asian child workers out there have gotten really demanding, you know. Very unrealistic expectations about remuneration. They've priced themselves out."

"'Priced themselves out?'"

"Exactly. Disabled people are much more competitive."

Martha took a deep breath. "But you stuck with the last project for a much longer period. That was an investment fund."

"Yes," smiled Thorne. "Rose and Thorne LLP has been a huge success. We acquired some great companies, made some huge profits, we've really gone from strength to strength."

"You've been criticised, though, about asset-stripping. Rose and Thorne buys struggling companies and then sells them off in pieces to make a profit, leaving thousands jobless."

"That's a huge over-simplification – "

Martha put down her pen and picked up her smartphone. "You tweeted a few days ago that the people need to rise up against corrupt, self-interested politicians," she said, scrolling through her feed.

Thorne nodded. "That's right, Martha. This country is crying out for transparency and accountability."

"But you were a lobbyist for industries with questionable values, an asset-stripper and a fat cat, if you'll pardon the pun, that got sued - don't you think *you* might be exactly the sort of politician that you are campaigning against?"

Thorne rubbed his chin and glanced out of the window. "I don't think our followers see it that way. They see a successful businessman who can rescue this country from the turgid, economic mess it's in."

"What would you say to criticism that the online activity of your followers is creating an angry, intolerant Britain?"

Thorne scoffed. "Nonsense. That's just the rough-and-tumble of national debate."

"And the death threats? And the violence? Aren't you just emboldening a new generation of racists?"

Thorne picked up his phone and tapped the screen. "Let me introduce you to some of our leadership team who might be able to reassure you," he said. "Look, Martha – may I call you Martha?"

"You – you literally have been, this whole time."

"Great. Martha, look. We believe in freedom. Freedom of speech, freedom of thought. I can't control what thousands of people who *may or may not* vote BEEF do. The real question is this – why are people so angry? Why do people feel beaten and forgotten?"

The café door opened and a man and a woman made their way towards them, snaking between tables of hipsters with laptops and mothers with children drinking babycinos.

"Ah," said Thorne. "Here they are."

They sat down, and Martha smiled as genially as she could. The woman, dressed functionally in a simple trouser suit, smiled back through a gaunt, bloodless face. Martha was reminded of a skeleton.

"Let me introduce Alicia Rhodes, our head of communications," Thorne said. "She has an illustrious pedigree, being formerly a member of the National British Front, the English National Party, the English National Front, and the National Trust."

Alicia nodded. "I am still a member of the National Trust," she said.

Thorne gestured to the man who sat down at his right. "And this is Bart McClure, our chief of strategy. Bart has really been the driving force behind our new direction, it's fantastic, what he's done over the last couple of years."

Martha felt a chill. She knew exactly who he was. Bart McClure was the founder of *ThinkRight*, an alt-right website that had become a major nexus for far-right dialogue. *ThinkRight* described itself as a news outlet, but as far as Martha was concerned it wasn't journalism - journalism survives cursory fact-checking. *ThinkRight*'s cocktail of conspiracy theories, minority-bashing and personalised attacks on liberal politicians was something quite different.

"Hi Martha," said Bart, in a smooth American accent. "I'm a great fan of what you do at the *Chronicle*. Great to meet you."

"Bart, hi," nodded Martha. "So maybe you're the best person to pick up this conversation about social media – would you say you're winning the social media war?"

Bart waved for attention from a server. "Look," he said as one made his way over. "Social media is about who has the clearest narrative. The world's big, and complicated, and people don't have time for boring, long-winded political nonsense. Clear messages win. And our message is really clear."

"Well that's certainly true – and is that the principle behind your campaign, *Hashtag Really*?"

Bart ran his hand through a wave of long, centre-parted grey hair. Martha hadn't seen that hairstyle since the nineties. "I'm so glad you asked about that, Martha. We're capturing the exasperating, self-evident lunacy of social liberalism. You know, 'taking in 30,000 more refugees –

hashtag really?' 'Another attack on traditional family values – hashtag really?' It's been very effective."

Martha nodded. It had. "Traditional family values – is that a code? What do you mean by that?"

Bart shrugged. "Hey, look, we're just asking the question, right? It's an important question, and one every British citizen should be asking. Questions are a healthy part of democracy."

Martha was grateful for the pause as the server arrived and Bart turned to him to begin the delivery of his complex coffee order. Even a few seconds of talk with Bart McClure felt like dancing with an evil octopus. It was easy to lose track of what all the tentacles were doing.

She turned back to Thorne. "So, Excelsior, your book is out now – what's it called?"

"Right, that's right!"

"Ah yes, 'Right, That's Right,'" repeated Martha, writing it down.

"No, not 'Right, That's Right,' I meant that's right, it's out now."

"'That's Right?'"

"No, no – it's called 'Keep Right: The Right to be Right and All Right, Right? Right!'"

"Right."

"Right!"

Martha put down her pen, rubbed her face, and took a deep breath. "So, tell me more about, er, that."

"Ah! Mr Williams," bellowed Harold Fisk as Dillon and Dave shuffled into his office.

"Hi, Mr Fisk," smiled Dave.

Fisk leapt up and strode towards them. He was a tall, muscular man, fond of bright, red braces and colourful striped shirts. Fisk's auburn hair was long enough to form a mullet at the rear, which cowered behind his neck – presumably glad to be away from the full force of his face.

"Good to see you, Mr. Williams, good to see you!" Fisk seized Dave's hand and pumped it with vigour. "Glad you got my letter! Thanks for coming in at such short notice! And it's Harry to you, big fella. And who is this fellow?"

Dillon held out a hand, which Fisk seized with equal enthusiasm. "Dillon Ruben, party secretary."

"I'm Harold Fisk!" he boomed, triumphantly. "Now, we need to talk, you boys and me! Ryan!"

"Yes, Mr. Fisk?" replied his receptionist, from outside the office.

"Cancel my two o'clock!"

"You haven't got one."

"Excellent! Gentlemen, to business!"

Fisk gestured to his desk, and Dave and Dillon sat down in comfortable, leather chairs. Fisk marched over to a long, oak bookshelf.

"Now, do you boys like scotch?"

"Er – it's a bit early for me, I'm fine, thank you," said Dillon.

Dave, nursing a hangover, also refused.

"Splendid!" beamed Fisk, punching a button on the wall. With a whirr, one of the bookshelves opened to reveal the sparkling collection of glass that was a well-appointed drinks cabinet. He pulled the cork out of a bottle of single malt and threw the contents into three glasses, two of which seemed to appear instantly in Dave and Dillon's hands. Within moments, Fisk was sprawled across his big, leather chair with his feet on his desk, slugging the whisky and grinning at his client.

Dave looked around, wondering whether five seconds or five minutes had just elapsed.

"Well," said Fisk, tipping his glass slightly towards Dave. "You're a lucky boy, aintcha?"

"Exactly which Cambridge college did Fisk go to, Dave?" whispered Dillon.

"Yes – yes I am," said Dave.

"Ten mil," whistled Fisk. "Ten damn mil. Ten damn mil pounds. Damn it, that sounds good."

"Yes, yes, it does."

"So! I suppose you two are wondering what the catch is!" Fisk chuckled.

"Catch?" replied Dave, exchanging a glance with Dillon.

Fisk's face darkened, and his smile drained away. He placed his glass on the desk, and leant towards them. When he spoke, his voice was low and gravelly.

"You have to spend a night in a haunted mansion," he said.

Dave and Dillon looked at each other.

"Gotcha!" boomed Fisk. "Ha, ha, ha! Damn, your faces! You guys are a hoot!"

Dave laughed nervously.

"Seriously," rasped Dillon under his breath. "Which college?"

Fisk downed the rest of his whisky and opened a manila file on his desk. "Okay, the small print," he said. "Now, this guy Mortimer's toast. I guess he was a big fan or something, so he's left you pretty much his entire estate. None of it's in property or anything like that, it's all cash. Looks to me like you'll be cleaning out his bank accounts. So, post-deductions, it's a cool ten million, ready to transfer from his shiny, sexy big-city account to whatever backwater peasant building society you guys have your party funds in."

"Party funds?" said Dave. "It can't be paid to, you know, one of us - personally?"

"Nope, sorry big man. This endowment is a legacy to the Happening Happy Hippy Party, not whichever motley crew happen to be sailing in her at the time. It all needs to be spent in pursuit of the HHHP's aims and objectives. Hell, though, if you guys vote yourselves big flashy cars or decide that fact-finding missions to the Bahamas count as party expenses, then live it up. But the money has to be accounted for through the HHHP. Now, this is your lucky day, because it just so happens that I have political experience. If you guys are looking for legal counsel then – look no further!"

"Sure," said Dillon. "But I'd like to know a bit more about Winstanley Mortimer. We've never heard of him. He's never been a member of the party. Who is he? Doesn't he have family to leave this money to?"

"It's funny you should ask that. See, normally with this sort of thing I have a lovely chat with the deceased's lawyers. But when I spoke to Plumpton and Bradley they didn't seem to know very much about him. Said he'd only instructed them the week before he died."

"And no family?"

"Apparently not. But hey, maybe you guys touched him with one of your campaigns or something. Or maybe he found you on the internet. Does it matter? You guys have one of the biggest political war chests in the country now. You're batting with the big boys! So, you're going to need some help. Let me pose you a little question, David. Can I call you David?"

"Um - "

"Suppose you wake up one morning, David," Fisk got up

and walked over to the window. Rain tapped gently against the glass. "You put on your little slippers, and down you pop to the front door to collect the newspaper. It's nice, and crisp, and fresh. 'I shall just catch up with the news of the day,' you say to yourself. Do you read the papers?"

"Yes - "

"So, you pick it up, and you're thinking, I'll go back to bed, sit up, have some nice coffee, bit of toast, nice relaxing morning – but shit, shit what's that on the front page? What the hell is that? 'David Williams,' it says, 'David Williams in Cocaine Sex Romp Orgy'!"

Dave grinned. "That sounds – oh no, oh right, I see. Oh dear."

"'Damn,' you think. Now that's not going to be true, is it? That's lies, David, lies uttered by your evil opponents. Maybe those fascist bastards, what are they called, Ham or something?"

"BEEF," said Dillon.

"Yeah, them. They've gone and briefed the Daily Bastard and there's your name on the page, for your missus, and party, and voters, and granny to read. They're all in their dressing gowns up and down the country, thinking, 'that David Williams, dirty little man.' Even your gran. She's looking down at her womb and cursing it for its role in the parade of obscenity that's led to this moment."

Fisk slapped his hand on Dave's shoulder, moving his face so close to Dave's that he could smell the whisky. "What's the answer, David? What do you do? 'Cocaine Sex Romp Orgy' – you don't want that, do you?"

Dave almost nodded, but caught himself and shook his head instead. "Er, no, no I don't want to have a Cocaine Sex Romp Orgy."

"The answer," whispered Fisk, "is to sue the bastards."

He leapt up, stabbing his finger in the air. "Sue, sue and sue some more! Sue the bastards, their children, their parents, their kids, their neighbours! And for that, you need a lawyer – a damn good one – with a Cambridge degree on his wall! David, you need Harold Maximillian Vito Fisk III, I thank you!"

Fisk threw himself over the desk and plunged into his chair. He sat in silence, a satisfied smile indicating that his case was made.

After a lengthy pause, Dillon was the first to speak. Dave was still thinking about the Cocaine Sex Romp Orgy.

"What Cambridge college did you go to, Mr. Fisk?"

"Cambridge College of Law, Lagos, Nigeria," he boomed. "The Internet, eh? What a time to be alive."

"We'll have you," said Dave.

Dillon's head spun round so quickly his neck almost snapped.

Dave stared back. "Cocaine Sex Romp Orgy," he mouthed.

THE EIGHT-TWENTY from London Waterloo clattered into Portsmouth Harbour railway station. The carriage doors slid open, and the salty scent of sea air swirled into Amy's nostrils. She stepped out into cold drizzle, grimacing as she walked along the platform.

"Portsmouth Harbour, this is Portsmouth Harbour," an automatic announcement interrupted the squeal of seagulls. "This train terminates here. All change, please. All change."

End of the line. End of the country, she thought, as she hurried for shelter under the concourse roof. Ducking out of the rain, she tried to reassemble her hair and shake the worst of the water out of her suit jacket. She sighed as she looked down to see that her elegant, magenta shirt had become soaked in moments. She coughed, and looked around for a taxi rank to the low rumble of thunder.

The railway station was built, somewhat unnervingly, over the harbour on enormous concrete stilts. The greeny-grey murk of the tide slithered moodily underneath, clearly visible below the train tracks. The masts of a Victorian steamer, HMS Warrior, rose proudly behind the station and the sound of tinkling nautical apparatus drifted across the concourse from the boats moored nearby.

"Portsmouth Harbour station," said Amy to herself, staring down at the dark wetness below. "They weren't kidding."

She made her way past the big Edwardian clock that presided over the station and to the exit, wheeling her smart, roller suitcase behind her.

Twenty-nine year old Amy Cordell had not expected this when she graduated six years ago with a First in Politics, Philosophy and Economics. Politically active on the university campus, the natural choice for her had been a career in and around Parliament. She had imagined, however, that this would entail lunching with journalists and lobbying MPs over quiet drinks in comfy Westminster pubs. She had not considered that it might involve hurrying through the rain in a seaside town to infiltrate a gang of largely-unemployed hippies.

Amy had felt a curious blend of pride and anger when the Prime Minister approached her with this assignment. Pride, because she had worked hard at the party headquarters week in, week out – pulling fifteen-hour days and sacrificing any glimmer of a social or romantic life. The first of the rewards for her work and talent had been her appointment to the Downing Street press office. This display of trust in her, perhaps, was the second.

But anger too, because it was impertinent and dangerous. Was she so loyal that if she was told to inveigle herself into another political party then she would, without question? No matter how illegal, how unethical, how scandalous it was?

No, it wasn't loyalty, she thought as she arrived at the steps out of the station and peered through the gloom for a taxi. It was ambition. Get this right, get the government re-elected, and Starling's job would be hers when he moved on. Only a few weeks in this godforsaken, seaweedy rockpool and it would be back to Downing Street for champagne and canapés.

Amy found a taxi and climbed inside, dropping down into the warmth of the back seat.

"Morning, love," said the driver, folding up his newspaper. "Where to?"

She glanced at her phone, and, as if trying to pronounce a foreign word, said: "Um, Sandport, please?"

The driver chortled from deep within his beer gut. "That'll be a bit pricey, love. See, it's the other side of the harbour. Long way by car."

"But I thought this was the closest station?"

"It is, sweetheart, it is – but the locals take the ferry."

"The ferry?"

The taxi driver pointed a sausage-shaped finger at the grey soup of the harbour. Something metallic and green bobbed up and down next to a pontoon that rolled unsteadily on the waves.

Amy followed the line of his finger, and sighed.

DAVE RAPPED on the coffee table with his front door key. "I call this meeting of the HHHP leadership to order," he said. "There are only two items on the agenda today – whether I do an interview with Coastal FM this afternoon, and how we spend ten million pounds."

They were back in HHHP Central, sprawled on the two sofas and sipping tea. Dave had wondered, as he unlocked it that morning, what would be the first thing they changed about their faithful old headquarters. Would the eclectic collection of political posters on the walls be the first to go? Or the comfortingly familiar sofas and beanbags, all draped in tie-dyed throws? A new teapot, maybe?

"Dillon, would you take the minutes?" he asked.

"Roger, roger," replied Dillon, pulling a pen and paper out of nowhere. Maybe he kept such things in his generous hair, thought Dave.

"Right, item one, the interview. Should we – "

"Yes!" said everyone in chorus.

"Okay, great, now, item two – "

"I have an idea!" said Rufus.

"Right, okay – let's start with your ideas then, Rufus."

"I think we should get a Playstation," he said.

"Er – well, we could do that Rufus. But we've got ten million quid here, shall we think more broadly than Playstations?"

"Oh, right, yes," replied Rufus. "Xbox?"

"I've come up with some ideas," said Catie, scratching her head and producing a sheet of paper from her satchel with the other hand.

"Great!" said Dave. "Go ahead."

"Well, I think we should start funding worthwhile causes. We shouldn't keep all this money to ourselves."

Dave nodded. "Yes, that sounds good – you know, one or two charities. Maybe ten percent or so of the cash."

Catie shook her head. "No, I meant about half the money. And I mean worthwhile *political* causes. I've made a list. Tree Liberation Front, the Fruitarian League – "

"Er, hang on there, Catie," interrupted Dave. "Half the money?"

"What's the Tree Liberation Front?" asked Rufus.

"They rescue trees from captivity, from the pens that farmers use to rear them, and re-plant them safely in forests."

"Where they can roam free?" smiled Dillon.

"I think that's criminal damage," said Rufus. "I don't think we should be a party that funds crime. They have names for those."

"Ha, ha – funding tree-rorism!" said Dillon.

Catie was wearing the tight-lipped, impassive look of which Dave had learned to be wary over the years.

"We're not saying that it's a bad idea," he said, quickly, in an effort to make the look go away. "But half the money might be a bit much. Maybe we can incorporate some of these organisation's ideas into our manifesto?"

"The manifesto is fine as it is!" blurted Rufus.

"I'm afraid that's not acceptable," said Catie, joylessly. She laid down her sheet of paper. "If we are truly committed to the hippy ideal then we must commit to the freedom of all living things."

Dave sighed. "I'm not disagreeing with that, I just think that if we were to win the election then it might be a bit difficult to persuade the Department for the Environment, Food and Rural Affairs to come round to the idea of free-range trees."

Catie folded her arms. "We'll they'll just have to. I want to give some money to the Tree Liberation Front."

"Maybe we could invite the Tree Liberation Front to come and talk to us about their work, and maybe we could see if there's a way we could incorporate some of their objectives into the party?"

"Would we give them funding?"

"I really don't think we can give them money to break into places and take trees, but perhaps we could provide funds for them to continue their work in a more legal way."

"Yes, they could branch off into other things," smiled Dillon. "You know, tackle the issue at the root."

Catie ignored Dillon and turned this over in her mind. "Yes, I suppose that would be all right. You want to meet the Tree Liberation Front?"

"Putting it in the minutes," said Dillon. "HHHP to liaise with the TLF to see if we can help them turn over a new leaf."

"I'll ask him when he's free," said Catie, picking up her piece of paper again.

"Sorry," said Dave. "*Him*? There's only one of them?"

"Yes," replied Catie. "TLF is my mate Steve."

Dillon put down his pen and looked up. "There's a bigger question here, Dave. You said *if we were to win* the election. We haven't decided yet whether to fight this seat. Or to aim higher and fight every seat. Or to campaign at all."

"Even if we convinced every member of the party to stand for a seat, there wouldn't be enough to fight every seat," said Catie.

"How many party members do we have, exactly?" Asked Dave. "Rufus?"

"I'm glad you asked. Well, no, I'm not actually. I have no idea. I don't know how many party members we have. Fifty? Ten? Pick a number."

"Oh, great," said Dillon, sipping his tea.

Dave leaned back into the sofa. "How are we going to run an effective party machine if we can't even keep a proper membership list?"

"I have e-mail addresses," shrugged Catie. "And there are Twitter followers. And the Facebook group."

"Well, that's a start. And I think we *should* contest every seat. This is our chance, guys. We're never going to get an opportunity like this again. Don't you want to do something about the world? Don't you want to make a stand?"

"I do," said Catie. "Actually it was *your* desire to make a stand I wasn't sure about."

Dave turned to Rufus and Dillon. "And you guys?"

Dillon brushed his hair out of his face. "Look, I don't mean to be the cold voice of reason here, but I just want us to think clearly. Make a considered decision. We need to think about what we're getting into. Are you ready for this? Are you ready for the intrusion and the drama? We have no meaningful experience. We don't know anything about politics. Not really. What if we don't get taken seriously?"

"We can hire staff," said Dave. "Get some experts in to help us run things. You could have a whole department, Dillon. Rufus, a whole team of accountants, and a load of policy guys. Catie, a PR machine. What do you think? Rufus?"

Rufus cleared his throat. "Would any of them know how to use a spreadsheet? Because it might be a bit difficult if we all have to share the HHHP abacus."

Dave checked his watch. "Well, maybe we vote on it later

- we need to get off to the radio station. Rufus, you need to go to the bank about the money transfer."

"Right-o!"

"YOU'RE LISTENING TO COASTAL FM," enthused Danny Gray into the microphone. "This is the Danny Gray Show on a beautiful Tuesday afternoon!"

Danny punched a button on his console and a cheerful jingle confirmed that it was, indeed, the Danny Gray Show. "So, the election's coming up next month, right, Simon?"

"Yep," replied Danny's co-host from behind an impressive dashboard of dials and switches. "Only a few weeks 'til Britain goes to the polls."

"We thought that it might be fun to talk to one of our local parties about the issues important to the people of Sandport. We've got with us, here in the studio, Dave, Dillon and Catie, from the," Danny's eyes narrowed as he tried to read his notes. "The Happening Hippy Hope Party?"

"Er, that's Happening Happy Hippy Party," corrected Dave, leaning in too closely to the microphone and sending a bank of flickering lights on the wall into a flurry of activity.

"Yeah, sure, whatever, great to have you here, guys!"

The three were crammed into what was not much more than a hot little booth, elbow to elbow with Danny and Simon. The producer was visible through a small window, and most of the meagre wall space was taken up by a giant, colourful Coastal FM logo.

"It's great to be here, Danny," said Dave, as energetically as he could.

"So, you guys are one of these comedy parties, right? You've got hilarious policies, you pull crazy pranks. But we thought it might still be fun to talk about your take on what's really going on out there. What do you think is important to Sandport in this election?"

"Well, let me stop you there, Danny," replied Dave. "We're not a joke party, we're serious. And we really care about the people of Sandport, and of Britain. These are dark times. People have lost faith in government, in democracy maybe. And they need us."

"Er, okay," said Simon. "I'm confused. You have these funny policies, and don't always contest elections, and all that. Is this a joke or not? Are you joking, or are you a joke? Or maybe the joke everybody's laughing at is not the one you think you're making."

Danny was scrolling through the party's website on a tablet. "I've been reading some of your manifesto policies and, I've got to say, moving the whole country north? Honestly? How can you call yourselves 'serious'?"

Dave scrambled around in his mind for Rufus' explanation of the manifesto. "It's an, er, ironic, tour of – "

"So, you're going to sit here and tell us that the HHHP isn't joking, when your defence policy includes banning guns and giving the army big sticks to poke our enemies with?"

Dave glanced at Dillon for support, but the party secretary was biting his lip. It wasn't going well.

"Let's talk about how the major parties are failing," suggested Dave.

"Yeah, but the major parties at least have credible policies, no matter how unpopular," drawled Danny, in full flow now. "I mean, you guys turn up in your little campervan thing and sit here, telling us to disarm the military? In Sandport – a navy town? How many candidates are you even fielding? One? Shouldn't you be concentrating on local issues, things that matter to Sandport?"

"The campervan's a laugh, though, Danny," grinned Simon. "It looks like an antique. And not, like, one of the ones on those TV shows where they find expensive things in attics."

"The campervan is a symbol of the hippy movement," said Dave.

"Really? I was thinking less hippy movement and more bowel movement!" Simon cackled, and high-fived Danny.

Dave cleared his throat. "Actually Danny, we're fielding more than six hundred."

Danny's smile dissolved into incredulity. "Six *hundred*? But you need some serious funding for that. Do you have the money?"

"Yes. We do. You see *some* people believe in us. We have a campaign budget of ten million pounds, and we're going to use it to take on the government. And we're going to make them accountable. We're going to make this country work again. We're going to make everything okay."

Dave smiled inwardly. Danny's stunned silence at his announcement on live radio gave him the freedom of the airwaves. So, he continued.

"Our policies may not have been sensible before, Danny. Sure. But that was the right thing to do at the right time. But we've got a new strategy now. The question for your listeners is, are you ready for a new voice? A fresh voice, from a party with no sinister influences, no favours to pay back? Is it time for you to listen to the Happening Happy Hippy Party?"

Danny let a beat pass. "One of your economic policies is to reduce the deficit by having everybody check down the back of their sofas for loose change," he said.

"ONE OF YOUR economic policies is to reduce the deficit by having everybody check down the back of their sofas for loose change."

Amy turned the radio off and surveyed herself in the mirror of her modest hotel room. Tight t-shirt. Purple, boot-cut jeans. Spangly CND earrings. It felt wrong to wear such comfortable, casual clothes. What seemed like a lifetime in power suits meant that she had almost forgotten what it felt like. She'd had to buy it all new.

The earrings were too much, she concluded. She reached up into her long, dark brown hair and detached them.

"Hi," she said to her reflection. "I'm Amy. It's great to meet you."

Something was missing. She turned to her suitcase and pulled out a yellow bandana, which she tied on her head.

"Hi, I'm Amy. I'm so pleased to meet you."

She modelled herself from a few angles, and nodded. Perfect.

Amy closed the suitcase, collected her phone and purse, and made for the door. The Prime Minister's words echoed in the back of her mind. 'Your mission,' they said, 'is to make them electable.'

As she left the hotel room, she thought about the radio show, and just how difficult that mission might prove to be.

"ONE OF YOUR economic policies is to reduce the deficit by having everybody check down the back of their sofas for loose change."

"So those hairy, ozone-sniffing cretins have a serious election budget," said Thorne. "Turn it off, Bart."

Bart leaned over from the driving seat and turned off the radio. Alicia sat in silence for a moment as the Mercedes growled up the road, watching Sandport go by. It was better for Thorne to start the conversation. That way she could have the answers rather than the questions. It was always better to be the one with the answers.

"Do we have a problem, Alicia?" asked Thorne eventually.

She pursed her lips. "Probably not," she said. "This has been a safe Tory constituency for decades. The electorate can be encouraged to move a little along the spectrum to the right, but it would be a miracle if the HHHP could get them to move so far left that they fall off the spectrum, carry on past the bus-stop and go straight on 'til morning."

"I hear you," said Bart. "But the Tory vote here was built on Peter Massingbird's personal popularity. That's why we're in with a chance. Without Massingbird, there's no guarantee that this *is* a Tory constituency. What's to say that the HHHP doesn't strike a chord?"

Alicia felt a stab of annoyance, but inwardly changed gear. "I think an insurance policy might be wise, just in case they manage to make some headway," she said, as if that had been her conclusion all along.

Thorne nodded. "What do you have in mind?"

She smiled. "Leave it to me."

3

"Well, Dave," said Catie, as they climbed back into the campervan. "I think our next debate is going to be a big one."

Dave started the engine and reversed the van out of its slot in the Coastal FM carpark. "I made an executive decision," he said.

"You had no business making 'an executive decision'! We're supposed to vote on these things! Now you've committed us to a giant national campaign, and told the world that we have a huge budget!"

"The press will be all over us," said Dillon. "I expect they'll be back at HHHP Central, now. Bumping into Rufus, my goodness. Rufus is about to become the HHHP's point-person for our first serious media interest ever. *Rufus.*"

"Everybody just calm down," said Dave, as he eased the van out into the afternoon traffic. "We have to declare the donation anyway, and Catie, I thought you were in favour of a national campaign? That's what you said this morning."

"For goodness sake, Dave, it doesn't matter what I think – what matters is that we're supposed to *vote*!"

"Rufus," said Dillon, shaking his head.

"Oh, come on," sighed Dave. "We vote on *everything*. The content of the blog, who we follow on Twitter, what brand of tea we have at HHHP Central, who buys the beer – we can't behave like that anymore if we're going to be a serious party."

"We haven't even voted on whether we're going to be a 'serious' party!"

Dave glanced at Dillon. "Dillon, you said you'd support us fighting this seat."

Dillon shrugged. "I didn't say that. I said that the barrier was us having no money."

"But now we have money!"

"Well, does it have to be now? There's less than two months until the election, that's no time at all to build up enough support to make a dent. We'd blow the money. We'd be the shortest-lived flash in the pan since that Timmy Mallett song about bikinis. Instead, we could spend it on building infrastructure for the next four years. Grow the party. Or even bank it and use the interest. Parties take years, even decades, to establish."

"I can't believe I'm hearing this," said Dave. "We finally get a shot at the big time, in an age where our ideals need fighting for more than ever, and we're talking about *infrastructure*?"

"I'm just being pragmatic."

"BEEF are out in front of even the Tories, Dillon."

"Here, yes. But not nationally, right?"

"They're doing well enough for this election to really work for them," said Catie. "They're not going to win any other seats, but look at the growing support base."

Dave could feel something rising inside him. A fire, of

sorts. He wasn't sure whether it was passion, or anger, or frustration – but it was more than he'd felt in a long time.

"Guys," he said. "BEEF are out there now, the poster-boys for a cynical, right-wing hijack of a scene left vacant when, one by one, the major parties lost their credibility. Are you telling me we're just going to let them have it? Dillon, is that what you want?"

THE MERCEDES ARRIVED at BEEF's hustings for the afternoon, a modest stand erected on the busy shopping precinct outside Sandport's town hall. Alicia briefly inspected it from her seat in the car. Activists handing out leaflets, banners in the right places with 'BF' and '#Really' emblazoned on them, a small dais with a microphone for Thorne – all seemed in order. A small crowd had gathered around a literature display, and there was no sign of irritating protesters. The morning's rain had gone, replaced by bright, spring sunshine.

"Okay," she turned to Thorne. "It looks good. Remember the key points of the speech. Be passionate, but not angry. Remember, they already secretly agree with us – you just have to reassure them that it's okay to vote for us, that it's not embarrassing to have these views."

"Values," said Bart from the front of the car, turning off the engine. "Not views – values. Sounds more noble."

Thorne gazed at the crowd with derision. "Look at them. The great unwashed. It would be a miracle they're out here at all, rather than slumped in front of *Big Wife Talent Factor Four,* if they didn't need to collect their giros and buy all their crisps and instant noodles. Is mediocrity contagious? I'm worried it's contagious."

Alicia glanced at the crowd. It was a pretty eclectic group, a cross-section of society. That was good. It would look great in the photos. "When you've given the speech, come down from the podium and shake a few hands. We've got security on hand just in case."

"I don't see any journalists," murmured Bart.

"Shake?" Snapped Thorne with visible disgust. "Do you have hand sanitiser? I want hand sanitiser for afterwards. I don't want to get poor-person on anything."

The theme from a TV soap about the White House rang through the car, and Bart put his phone to his ear. "Bart McClure. Oh, Martha, hi – I was just thinking about you! You know, Mr Thorne's giving a speech in a few moments, outside the town hall. You're going to want to go ahead and stop by, I think, there's going to be a good headline in it."

"Here," said Alicia, unearthing a small bottle of fluid from her handbag and handing it to Thorne.

"The who? The hippies?" said Bart into his phone, annoyance bleeding into his voice. "No, we don't feel threatened at all – who would? A bunch of washed-up hippies led by a narcissistic layabout, that angry lesbian, a backing dancer from a Marilyn Manson gig and Lord Titty McTitties of Tiny-Bollocks? No, Martha, we're not threatened. We're amused. This election needs a comedy sidekick. We look forward to exposing them on the hustings. Bye."

"Okay, it's time," said Alicia, and stepped out of the car.

"WELL, the screaming hordes of the press don't seem to have descended yet," said Dave, a note of disappointment in his voice as he pulled the van up outside HHHP Central. The last half of the journey had been completed in silence.

Wordlessly, Catie and Dillon left the vehicle and went inside to meet Rufus, Dillon stooping to do so, while Dave pulled up the handbrake and placed a brick underneath it to keep it in place. He climbed out of the van, grabbed a padlock from the driver side door pocket and used it to lock the campervan.

As he walked through the door into HHHP Central, he caught the tail-end of a conversation that he had predicted would be taking place.

"And that was that," Catie was telling Rufus. "El Presidente's diktat was complete."

Dave took a deep breath as Rufus looked at him.

"Wow," said Rufus.

"Look," said Dave. "Let me explain."

"You got a penis tattoo on live radio?"

Dave stopped. "What? What on earth are you talking about?"

"Catie just said it, a dick t – "

"No, Rufus," interrupted Dave. "She meant that I made a unilateral decision."

At that moment, and somewhat to Dave's relief, Catie's phone rang. She slipped it out of her pocket and raised it to her head.

"Catie Fitzgerald. Oh, hi Martha. Great to hear from you. Comment? On what? They called us *what*? Hang on, I'll put you on loudspeaker. Tell the whole party what BEEF called us."

She did, and she did.

"Our comment is this," said Catie, her voice firm. "Those few words expose exactly what BEEF stand for, and how they'll respond to anyone that stands in their way. And that's why the people of Sandport need to stop them."

Catie hung up, and the room was silent for a moment.

"Are you okay?" Dillon asked her.

She nodded, her face flushed. "Yeah, I'm fine. It's nothing more than we'd expect from them."

"Isn't there anything we can do about this?" asked Rufus.

"Yes," said Dillon. "We can stand. We can launch a national campaign."

Dave looked up. "Really? You're on board?"

"Yeah," replied Dillon with a smile. "Someone has to challenge that. And goodness knows the major parties aren't doing it."

"Me too," said Catie.

"And me," said Rufus. "Let's do it."

Dave beamed. "That's great! So we should – we should make a plan. We need to start planning the campaign."

"I think we need to do talking points first," said Catie. "A campaign plan is important, but the press *are* going to ask questions about our intentions imminently and we need to know what to say to them. We don't have much time."

"Okay, talking points," repeated Dave. "Talking points. We can set up some talking points. Talking points."

Catie's eyes narrowed. "You don't know what talking points are, do you, Dave?"

Dave shrugged. "Some kind of – board game?"

There was a knock at the door, and they fell silent.

"It's them," whispered Rufus. "*They've found us.*"

The door creaked open, and they found themselves staring at a female twentysomething in a bandana. Dave blinked. She was beautiful. Slim, dark-haired, with emerald eyes – for a moment, he thought she might look back at him, and their eyes might meet, and hold a gaze pregnant with hope, and romance, and adventure. But instead, her eyes glanced around their modest headquarters, and they only seemed to take in Dave in the way that they took in the posters and battered sofas.

"Hi," she said. "Is this – the HHHP?"

"Well hello," purred Rufus, standing up. "I'm Rufus, *very* pleased to meet you."

"Oh," said Amy, taking an instinctive step backwards. "Hi, I'm Amy. Pleased to meet you all too."

Dillon smiled. "Hi Amy, I'm Dillon, and you've come to the right place. We are indeed the HHHP. How can we help you?"

Amy shook Dillon's hand. "Hi, Dillon. Well, I found you guys online, and then I just heard your interview – I thought maybe I could help."

"Great!" said Dillon.

"What qualifications do you have?" asked Catie.

"Er, Catie – " began Dillon.

Catie folded her arms. "I just don't think we should be opening our door to strangers off the street like that."

Amy nodded. "I do have some experience that might be useful."

"Amy, you don't have to make an application," said Dillon. "It's always a pleasure to welcome a new member."

"No, it's quite all right, the lady is – aren't you, er...?"

"Catie."

"Well, Catie," Amy swallowed. "I've been in political public relations for six years, the last four years helping to run the Number Ten press unit. I managed relationships with several key national newspapers, helped to design two successive election campaigns and reported directly to the Number Ten director of communications."

There was a silence.

"Number Ten, like, in Number Ten Downing Street?" asked Rufus, sitting down.

"Yes," said Amy. "Number Ten Downing Street."

"Where the Prime Minister lives?"

"Well, no, the Prime Minister actually lives in Number Eleven," explained Amy. "It's more spacious than Number Ten and he has family."

Catie shrugged, but eyed Amy. "Well, I suppose that's something."

"Welcome aboard," said Dave, entering the conversation. "I'm Dave, I'm the party leader."

"Very pleased to meet you, Dave."

"Dillon is our party secretary, and Catie is our director of communications."

"I do the blog," said Catie.

"That's – very impressive," replied Amy.

"Sometimes I put pictures in."

"And this is Rufus, our treasurer," went on Dave.

"Actually," said Rufus, "it's The Honourable Rufus Lane-Seymour."

"Is that so?" asked Amy, with genuine surprise.

It was. Rufus belonged to Britain's long tradition of aristocratic eccentricity, favouring a collection of artisan suits in various shades of purple. He was born into the prestigious but reclusive Lane-Seymour family, which owned large swathes of Lancashire but operated behind a veil of darkness. This was largely unintentional, being mainly because internet search engines would automatically correct any searches to 'Jane Seymour'. It suited the family, however, as journalists curious about the activities they permitted on their land were diverted, while the famous actress often received probing questions from the press about hydraulic fracking on the Lancashire coast.

Rufus however, upon discovering the source of his family's revenue, had been horrified. He immediately attended his London club to remonstrate with his older brother, who controlled the family's interests, in an incident that onlookers described as a 'bit of a fuss'. Unable to change his brother's mind, Rufus had invited him to 'frack off' and charged out into the London night, never to be seen at the club again.

Seeking a better world, Rufus packed his necessities and only his most versatile sports jacket, and began a long pilgrimage on foot to India. As it happened, he discovered marijuana somewhere between Reading and Basingstoke and ended up circling Hampshire three or four times. Stumbling aboard a ship bound south from Portsmouth, Rufus found a quiet space near the bow to call home and erected a makeshift hammock.

When he was awoken by the crew forty-five minutes later and informed that he was, in fact, on the Isle of Wight ferry and alongside in Ryde, he wandered into the nearest bar and discovered Dave and Dillon on holiday.

"Yes," sighed Dave. "It's true."

"Government to the HHHP is a very big step," said Catie, walking to the kitchenette and putting on the official HHHP kettle. "A defection. Why?"

Rufus gestured to one of the sofas, and Amy sat down. "Well, I was just, you know – I got to thinking," she said. "About the party I was in. About the government, about the other parties. They've lost their roots, Catie. It's all spin, lobbying, lies, truth – I realised I was tired. *I've* lost my roots. I wanted to reach out for something fresh and new. And then I heard about you guys."

Catie retrieved mugs from a cupboard and set them on the worktop. "So, what are you doing for work now, Amy? If you've left your London job?"

Amy shrugged. "Nothing. I've got savings. I thought I'd

take some time out, you know? Do something that mattered to me."

"Well, we were just about to start planning the campaign," said Dave.

"Talking points!" Called out Catie from the kitchenette.

"Those too. You can help us. I mean, we haven't really done anything like this before."

Amy nodded. "You're going to fight a national campaign?"

"Yes, yes we just decided."

"Okay, well, wow. All right – you're going to need to do a lot very quickly, then. You need staff, volunteers, and a strategy. And a proper headquarters. This place is very cosy but you can't run a national campaign from here. And what's that smell?"

Dave waved his hand dismissively as Amy took out her phone and started tapping at the screen. "That's, er – "

"Who are your candidates?" She went on. "And your campaign team?"

"Um," said Dave. "We don't have any candidates yet. Well, apart from me. Probably. And the team – you're looking at them."

Amy stopped and stared at him.

"No candidates? At all?"

Dave shook his head.

Amy raised the phone to her ear. "Okay, well, I'll make some calls. There are people who owe me favours. But your priority right now is finding 649 viable candidates, because the deadline for nomination papers is the end of the week. So, can I suggest that two of you go out and start finding candidates, and two of you join me for some strategy brainstorming? Riz! Hi! Have you got five minutes?"

Dave nodded as Amy turned away to her phone call.

"Great. Okay, Dillon and Rufus – you're interviewing candidates. Put a shout-out on Twitter, Facebook, everywhere. Let's do this thing!"

They stared at him.

"Maybe I don't use the phrase 'let's do this thing'?"

They nodded.

There was another knock at the door, this time more commanding and accompanied by voices. There was movement in the bushes outside the window. Dave thought he saw a camera flash.

"Mr Williams? Mr Williams are you in there? Can you tell us a bit more about your party?"

"Are you really going to contest all the seats, Mr Williams?"

"Where'd the money come from, Dave? Can you pop out, just to say hi?"

"How do you think the British public will respond to you?"

"That really does sound like the press," said Dave.

"Hang on Riz," said Amy, putting the phone down for a moment. "It will be. We'll go away, Dave and Catie – I know a quiet place. A sort of, strategy retreat. We'll put out a short statement now saying that we'll do a press conference in a day or two. That should hold them off for twenty-four hours or so."

THE FOLLOWING MORNING, Dave and Catie sat at breakfast in a small, boutique hotel somewhere in the English countryside. Amy had arranged a car to collect them from HHHP Central – the press would have had no trouble following the campervan. And even if they did manage to lose them, the huge HHHP logo on the side – a big, pink flower with a stylised globe at the centre – would no doubt help them pick up the trail again.

Dave was grateful for the peace of the retreat. It had been a heart-pounding few days. A comfy bed, good coffee and the sound of birdsong drifting gently through the window were therapeutic.

"I don't like her," said Catie, jabbing her grapefruit. "I don't trust her."

"Why not?"

"I don't like her because she was barking orders at us before I had even finished making her a cup of tea. Seriously. And I don't trust her, because I don't see why someone from Number Ten would give it all up, just like that, and come all the way down to the toenail of Britain to join us. She's from a whole different world."

"Maybe she got tired of all the intrigue. You heard what she said – she's looking for her roots. We have a very broad appeal. Very earthy."

"Well, I don't like it. I'll be watching her."

"Shh, here she comes now."

"Morning guys," Amy said cheerfully, sitting down and helping herself to coffee. "How did you sleep?"

Dave smiled. "Great, thank you, really great."

"Perfunctorily," said Catie, without looking up. Dave blinked at her.

"That's wonderful," said Amy, grabbing a slice of toast. "I'm glad. This is a great place, isn't it? Beautiful, and so hard to find. Ideal to let the outside world go for a day or two, escape and do some really focussed thinking. Winston Churchill visited here once or twice, apparently. You can really feel the history crackling through the porticos and drawing rooms, right?"

Dave nodded and pretended to have his mouth too full to talk. He judged hotels on the contents of their complimentary coffee and tea making facilities. His most cogent thought about this place revolved around the quality of the individually wrapped shortbread.

"So, now you've both had a good night's sleep, have you had any thoughts about your campaign strategy?"

Catie took a sip of her tea. "Actually, yes. We need a big grassroots push, I think."

"I really agree," said Amy. "A big doorstep campaign. Lots of volunteers, lots of face-contact. The odds are stacked against you. The media will treat you like a skateboarding rabbit at the end of the news bulletin – a bit of comic relief. The best way to combat that narrative is to let people see your authenticity, first-hand."

"Exactly," said Catie.

Amy took a bite of toast and munched, thoughtfully. "So tell me," she said after she swallowed. "What is that message, exactly?"

"Our message?" said Dave.

"Well, you know - what do you stand for?"

Dave nodded. "Ah. Right, well – we stand for hope. For generosity, for inclusion. For social justice. For connecting to something greater than you. For equality. For freedom, for the joy of diversity, for social harmony and plurality."

"That's right," said Catie. "And for sustainability. For stewardship of the planet. For compassion. For co-operation, and integrity, and transparency. For challenging powerful vested interest. For promoting those who cannot promote themselves."

There was a brief pause.

"Okay," said Amy. "Look, those are great values, but they don't say anything tangible. They don't tell us what they *mean*. It just sounds like you've got Word of the Day toilet paper, George Monbiot edition."

"I don't see the problem," said Catie.

"The problem is that even BEEF could claim it agreed with all those principles. They're so basic, anyone can read anything into them. It's like cold-reading: 'I've got a message from the other side for someone who had an uncle with a name beginning with 'B', or maybe 'D', or maybe it's a brother-in-law, or other male relative?'"

"That's amazing," said Dave. "I've got a cousin called Derek."

Amy took a deep breath. "You've got a challenge here, guys. You not only need to get rid of that joke manifesto, but you need to replace it with something coherent that says *who* you are, *what* your solution is, and *how* you'll implement if it you win."

DILLON AND RUFUS sat at a table in Sandport community hall. Outside, prospective candidates waited patiently in the sun for their opportunity to explain why they should stand for the HHHP.

Catie's online outreach had been very successful. More successful, in fact, than any of them thought it would – but that was partly because an autocorrect typo in the advert ('candid dates') made it resemble a lonely-hearts classified, and it was interpreted as an ironic meme. It went viral within an hour.

"Okay Rufus," said Dillon, taking a sip of tea and opening his folder of notes. "Let's see the first candidate."

Rufus walked over to the door and opened it.

A man in a long, green raincoat and sandals shuffled

into the hall. Dillon watched Rufus' nose wrinkle as a thick stench of body odour, marijuana and excrement lay in the man's wake, hovering over a trail of dried mud and grass behind him. Long, unkempt auburn dreadlocks coiled around his shoulders like fat tubers. He walked over to a chair in front of the table, sat down, and grinned through a billowing ginger beard.

"Dolphin," he said, through sticky, yellow teeth.

There was a pause while Dillon and Rufus surveyed the apparition before them.

"Good morning, Mr Dolphin," said Dillon, slowly.

"Yeah, fine," said Dolphin. "Mind if I smoke, mate, yeah?"

"Well, there are no-smoking signs up all over the hall, I'm afraid," replied Dillon.

"Brilliant, yeah," said Dolphin, reaching into the dreadlocks and producing a crudely hand-rolled cigarette. He lit it with a plastic lighter and took a deep drag.

"So, yeah," he said.

Dillon wasn't quite sure what this sentence was supposed to mean, so he nodded to Rufus to ask the first question.

"Thank you for coming in, Mr Dolphin," began Rufus.

"No," snapped Dolphin. "It's just 'Dolphin'. No 'mister' here, mate. 'Mister' is one of the devices that the capitalist regime uses to subjugate us, yeah? It's like, a rank, yeah? A title, it shows you're one of *them*, yeah?"

Rufus glanced at Dillon and then back at Dolphin, who offered no further information about who 'they' were.

"All right, Dolphin it is. So, Dolphin, why do you want to stand as a candidate for the Happening Happy Hippy Party?"

"Well," said Dolphin, crossing his legs in a manner that

suggested to Dillon that this explanation might be quite
lengthy. "It's, like, the big war against the machine, yeah?
See, it's like, yeah, the establishment have got everything
stitched up, yeah? The courts an' the capitalists an' the
police an' the banks an' we gotta work together to smash the
system, yeah? Like, the Bilderbergers an' the UN an' the
World Bank an' the EU an' the USA an' Parliament, and
everyone, got it all set up and they're destroying the world,
right? And we gotta stop them, rising up like Che Gevurera,
an' bring powers to the streets, man, yeah? Down in here in
the streets, where we can rule from, and yeah?"

There was another pause while Dillon assessed whether
Dolphin had concluded his assessment with a rhetorical or
actual question.

"So," he said. "Why do you want to stand as a candidate
for the Happening Happy Hippy Party?"

"I just told you, didn't I?" replied Dolphin, throwing his
dreadlocks back over his shoulders. "Yeah?"

"Right, okay, well, thank you – thank you for sharing
your thoughts with us there," said Dillon. "So, what sort of
constituency would you hope to represent, and how would
you approach being an MP if you were elected?"

Dolphin took a thoughtful drag on his cigarette.

"Well, yeah, it's like, the global village, innit? We're all
the same, we're all part of the karma force. You me, *them* –
but the establishment an' the banks an' the police an' the
government an' the USA, they're all, like, unbalancing the
karma with dark karma, an' we gotta rise up like Che Gulev-
erla as one, yeah? Got to throw off the chains of oppression,
yeah?"

Rufus coughed as the cigarette smoke clouded around
him. "Can you tell us what sort of experience you'd be able
to bring to the party?"

"Not much mate, I've been in a tunnel for the last nine months under the third runway site at Heathrow."

Dillon slapped his folder shut. "Thanks for coming in, Dolphin."

DAVE, Catie and Amy had spent the morning in one of the hotel's conference rooms, mapping out their campaign strategy. They didn't stop for lunch, munching on sandwiches while they prioritised constituencies and organised a timetable.

Amy had been on and off her phone throughout the day, arranging meetings and speaking events, reserving advertising space, securing computers and buses and goodness knew what else. She had pulled in favours far and wide, and made a fresh bank of promises. Dave was fascinated to watch her work. This was how things happened. It seemed effortless, deft - he was impressed.

In every conversation, however, it was not long before they came back to the huge, immovable barrier that was their manifesto. And now, in the early afternoon, Dave and Amy stood with mugs of tea, surrounded by huge sheets of flipchart paper and portable whiteboards covered in a multicolour graffiti of arrows, sticky notes and diagrams. Catie had folded herself up on a cushioned banquette beneath a bay window, looking out over the hotel's gardens.

"I'm still not sure," murmured Dave as he sipped.

Amy looked at him. "About what?"

"I mean, this is all great – really, really great – but how are we *different*, if we have all these clever plans? Everybody's got clever plans. How do we stand out?"

"Are you kidding? You are the *most* different thing on the menu this election, Dave."

"Really?"

"Look, professional politicians seem remote and insincere. Right-wingers seem elitist and cruel. Left-wingers seem sanctimonious and idealistic. Everybody's striving for one particular thing, the one magic ingredient that the electorate invariably rewards. None of them have it, but you do. You have it in quantities I've never seen before."

"What?" asked Dave. "What is it that we have?"

"It's what we're going to build your campaign around. It's your secret weapon, the Holy Grail, the MacGuffin."

"The Mawhattin?"

Amy shrugged. "Isn't it obvious?" She grabbed a marker and scrawled 'AUTHENTICITY' on the last white space of the last whiteboard.

She took a step back and turned back to them. "People are so desperate for authenticity in their politicians that they'll tolerate a liar, because they *know* he's a liar. You guys are *real* and honest. And you're going to have a message that can compete with what BEEF's putting out. It'll be simple, it'll be clear – BEEF might be asking 'the question' – you've got the *answer*. You just have to decide what it is," she added.

Catie uncurled herself from the window. "We are real," she said. "But BEEF is just drawing out all the natural, deep prejudices hidden in people. And the main parties are getting in on the act. How do you compete with that?"

"No," said Amy, shaking her head. "They're not natural, and they're not deep. People are complicated. Most minds are a battleground. The people who are sympathetic to BEEF – it doesn't come from inbuilt racism. It comes from fear. They've got big questions and don't know what the answers would look like. And the far-right have an advantage, because they have simple answers that fit neatly into 140 characters. That's why the major parties are echoing them."

"But in reality, there are so many moving parts that meaningful solutions have to be nuanced," said Catie. "And nuance is the first casualty of mass media."

"And that's what you guys need to tackle, Catie," replied Amy, putting down her mug. "Look, let's head back to base. We can start the campaign now, and keep it general – but you need to get a manifesto, a doctrine even, together. Urgently. Like, in a couple of days. We can generate interest in you now, but people need to know what you actually stand for in order to give you their vote."

"Ready for the next one, Rufus," said Dillon.

Rufus opened the door, and a tall, muscular young man in a skin-tight t-shirt strode in. Shiny military boots and olive combat pants carried him over to the chair, on which he sat without saying a word and stared at Dillon.

Dillon looked him up and down. The shaved head was not alarming in itself, and neither was the lip-piercing or the stud in one ear. The tattoo of an eagle carrying a red, flaming swastika on one arm, and the word 'cristolnakt' on the other, however, enabled Dillon to predict how this interview was likely to go.

"Hi," said Dillon. "I'm Dillon."

The man, who had not blinked once since arriving, nodded. "Hello."

"I don't seem to have your name on my list," said Dillon.

"Quentin," he said.

"Well, thanks for coming in, Quentin," said Rufus.

"Would you like to tell us why you think you should be a candidate for the Happening Happy Hippy Party?"

There was a pause while Quentin digested this.

"Got to promote the hippy ideal and all that," he said, finally. "Got to give the foreigners all the benefits and bring in all the immigrants so that they can have all the British jobs, 'cos that's good, right?"

"Er, if you're saying that we believe in social justice, equality and freedom of movement then yes, those are very HHHP things."

Quentin grunted, apparently satisfied that he had said enough.

"Quentin, I've got a question,' said Dillon. "I don't suppose you've belonged to any other political parties, have you?"

Quentin jumped to his feet. "No! No I ain't in no other party! Where did you get that lie? Who told you that? No, I want to join the HHHP and keep the Jews in power! You can't prove nothing, right? You ain't got nothing!"

Dillon and Rufus sat in silence for a moment, watching Quentin's powerful frame heave up and down, his face raw with fury.

"Let me put this another way," said Dillon. "You are in another party, and that other party is BEEF, and this is about as convincing an infiltration attempt as a killer whale trying to get into a goldfish wedding."

Quentin kicked the chair over. "You're finished, hippy bastards," he roared. He pointed at his t-shirt. "This is the big year, you know, this is it! We got the American government, we're booting out the invaders of this island, and you're all gonna regret everything when we run the country!"

Dillon stood and gestured to the door. "I expect I might

be more convinced by this if you could actually spell 'Kristallnacht,'" he said, nodding to Quentin's arm.

Quentin stormed through the door and thundered past the other candidates waiting outside with a tirade of exotic expletives.

Dillon called after him from the doorway. "I suggest that you go back to BEEF headquarters and tell Excelsior Thorne he's going to have to try harder than that to get his cronies into the HHHP!"

He turned to the other candidates. "The rest of you. If any of you are BEEF infiltrators you can also pick up your stuff and move along! Get out of here!"

Half of those present stood up and left, their chains and piercings clinking as they went.

DILLON AND RUFUS sat in their own sweat, the next candidate taking her seat before them. Their sleeves were rolled up and their mouths were dry, a battalion of empty tea mugs littering the table. The scent of frustration and fatigue hung in the air, unmoved by the inadequate fan that twirled uselessly on the ceiling.

It had been a long day.

Dillon brushed lank hair out of his face and fixed the candidate with his gaze. She smiled back.

"Are you a fascist?" He said.

"No."

"Are you mental?"

"No."

"Are you wanted by the police?"

"No."

"Do you actually know what the Happening Happy Hippy Party is?"

"Yes – of course."

He slammed his palm on the table. "You're in. Pick a constituency. Next!"

"WELL, I thought it went very well," said Alicia.

She and Thorne sat at a small table in the Boatman's Arms, the pub that had become BEEF's de-facto second headquarters. Thorne frequented the Boatman because it served real ale, had a politically sympathetic landlord, and because he or his party were barred from almost every other pub in town.

Alicia approved of his patronage here, however, as it helped to support his image as a happy, political outsider taking on the establishment and in touch with the man in the street. Photos of Thorne drinking beer gave him a blokey, everyman appeal – laughing with ordinary, local people. Of course, he required encouragement to laugh with ordinary, local people. At least forty per cent of such photos actually showed him laughing *at* ordinary, local people.

Thorne was not doing much laughing now, however, as they both reflected on the morning's campaigning – a tour around a local automotive parts manufacturer.

"It didn't go bloody well at all," replied Thorne. "Not at all."

"No, I think it was fine. The owner was very on-side, very on-message."

She glanced at Bart, who sat at a different table, clattering away on a laptop computer with a mostly-untouched sparkling mineral water beside him. It would be nice to have his support with wrangling Thorne, she thought, at least every once in a while.

"Yes but his bloody foreign workforce wasn't, Alicia! Didn't we vet the place?"

"Of course, and that's exactly why we chose it. We need lots of coverage of you being nice to foreign workers, showing how wonderfully approachable we are. That's how we keep our immigration policy from looking nasty and toxic."

"I don't care," growled Thorne. "I get to choose who I meet next, I don't want my hands smelling of bloody garlic sausage again. No bloody foreigners."

"Right," sighed Alicia, taking out a pen and making a note. "No more foreigners."

"Or babies. I hate babies. All bubbly noses and whimpering."

"Okay, sure. No babies," said Alicia, adding babies to her list.

"Or children. I don't have time to waste on ankle-biters who won't be able to vote for me for a decade."

"No children. Got it."

"Or construction workers. Elderly people. The disabled."

"Okay."

"Long-term sick. Bankers. Shopkeepers. Bin men. Council workers, bakers, soldiers, students."

"None of those," said Alicia, scribbling hard to keep up.

"Computer programmers, journalists, teachers, nurses, firemen, butchers, supermarket workers, mechanics, sailors – "

A notification on Alicia's phone emitted a ping.

"Engineers, clergymen, bloody musicians, photogra-

phers, bus drivers, doctors, career advisors, consultants, air
hostesses, taxi drivers, IT engineers, charity workers – "

"Anybody else?"

"And no bloody farmers, either."

Alicia looked down at the notification. There was a new
article on *ThinkRight*, with the title 'is the HHHP everything
that's wrong about Britain?' Alicia glanced at it, noting that
woven into its various allegations were Twitter handles and
e-mail addresses.

Bart was sending in the trolls.

IT WAS GETTING dark as the car squirmed through the
evening traffic, returning to Sandport. Dave wasn't used to
quiet, clean motorised transport with comfortable seats.
Perhaps Catie wasn't either, and that was why she had fallen
asleep almost immediately on his shoulder. Amy sat in the
front passenger seat, still stabbing away furiously at her
phone.

"Wait," said Dave, looking out of the window. "This is
the wrong way. This isn't the way to HHHP Central."

"No," said Amy, turning around to face him. She
grinned. "This is the way to your new campaign headquarters."

She had scarcely finished speaking as the car escaped
from the glut of traffic and swooped past Sandport town
hall, pulling up outside a modern office development.
Diamond-shaped timber frames criss-crossed a fascia of
mint-green glass, as creeping plants billowed out of window
boxes. It stood directly opposite the town hall, in sharp
contrast to the functional concrete of the hall's sixties archi-
tecture.

"Welcome to Green House," she said. "I thought you guys should have the most environmentally-friendly building available in Sandport."

"Golly," said Dave, as a clutch of journalists and photographers descended on the car. The interior of the car lit up in flickering camera flashes, and a dozen hands tapped on the windows.

"Just smile and say 'good evening'," said Amy, unbuckling herself. "Don't say anything else for now and get inside as quickly as you can."

She opened the door and stepped out, while Catie – who had been roused from her sleep by the activity – did the same. Dave took a deep breath, steadied his nerves, and followed.

"Good evening," he tried to smile in the blinding white lights. "Lovely to see you, thank you."

He realised that he couldn't even see the door to Green House in the tumult of people and flickering lights. It was like a nightclub, and not a good one. Just as his disorientation was about to lead him off in the wrong direction he felt Amy's reassuring hand take his arm, and charge him through the crowd.

"Just look this way for a moment please, Mr. Williams," shouted someone.

"Dave, Dave do you really think you can win a seat?"

"You have the third-biggest electoral budget in the country, Mr Williams, what do you have to say about that?"

"Over here, Mr Williams!"

Electric doors slid open to welcome them into the peace of the lobby, while two burly security guards kept the crowd at bay with their stares and chests alone.

"Phew," said Dave. "They're keen."

A chinstrap-bearded Asian man in his mid-thirties,

dressed in a fashionable shirt and jacket was waiting patiently for them. He held out his hand to Dave.

"Mr Williams," he said. "Great to meet you. Riz Islam."

"Hi, Riz," said Dave, shaking his hand. "It's Dave. And, um, who are you?"

"I'm your chief of staff," smiled Riz. "Welcome to HHHP campaign headquarters. Let me give you a tour."

Riz shook Catie's hand too, and embraced Amy, before leading them out of the lobby.

"This is a great building for the HHHP to lease," he said as he used a pass-card to admit them through electronically-secured doors. "Built with renewable plant materials and recycled metal and concrete, solar panels, water efficiency – any dishwashing water is used to flush the toilets."

Riz took them up some steps and into a wide, open-plan office, smiling and nodding at people as he went. Big, flat-screen televisions were suspended from the ceiling, beaming twenty-four-hour news channels into the office. The aroma of organised chaos hung in the air as phones and computers were unpacked from cardboard boxes, and people scurried around with notebooks in their hands or phones at their ears.

"The funds are going in three main directions," said Riz. "Or three prongs to the campaign, if you like. Co-ordinated local campaigns, which have government-imposed spending restrictions, like Sandport. Then the national campaign, and then the digital campaign. All are important."

Headsets and computers littered the first set of desks they came to.

"This is the phone-bank management suite," said Riz. "This is one of the ways we'll be reaching out to people."

"It doesn't seem very big," said Dave.

"It's just the management suite," replied Riz. "The actual phone bank is virtual – we'll be using software so that phone operators can work from their own homes. That way people with restricted mobility, or care commitments, or children and so on can participate and we can keep costs low. We have some workstations here for those who would prefer not to work in their dwelling."

"'Dwelling'?"

Riz glanced at Amy. "Well – not everybody sleeps in a place they'd want to stay in during the day, of course."

"Oh, right, yes," nodded Dave, a little over-emphatically. He pointed to a larger set of desks, behind which stood a huge whiteboard with a big map of Britain. "And what's that bit?"

"That's the first prong of the campaign – that's where all the local constituency campaigns will be supported from," said Riz. "Whatever they need, any issues they have, any messages we want to put out to them – those guys will sort it out."

"I don't know any of these people," whispered Dave to Catie.

Riz overheard. "They're from the university, mostly," he said. "Mainly political science students, eager to build experience. Keen to help out. But as the support mounts we'll get more ideologically-motivated volunteers."

They arrived at a glass-walled meeting room that stood in the centre of the office like an aquarium.

"Ah," said Riz, as he opened the door. "Here's some familiar faces."

Dillon and Rufus sat at a long meeting table looking up at a smart-board that was divided into hundreds of coloured panels, like a giant pixelated rainbow. A man in a crimson fedora hat, white scarf and wide-necked t-shirt was scribbling words on a flipchart. He spun around.

"Hello!" he said in a strong German accent. "I am Gunther!"

"Hi, Gunther," said Dave. "I'm Dave."

Gunther sprinted over to him, and furiously shook his hand. "I am so very pleased to meet you, David Williams! What a pleasure it is to be here, at the beginning, the inception, the very start of something so big and important!"

"Well that's, yes – so, what are we doing in here?"

"We are choosing an official party colour," said Dillon, with an eyebrow raised. "It turns out that there are more than sixty shades of green alone."

"Gunther is a political colour consultant," explained Riz.

"My work, David Williams, is to make your brand, your platform, *explode* with meaning! I can make your party burst in the minds of the electorate, like a delicious fruit that splatters on the inside of their skulls!"

"With – colours?"

"Not just any colour, David Williams, but the right colour, the perfect colour, the ideal colour for the Happening Happy Hippy Party!"

"Do we need a colour?" asked Catie. "We use psychedelic a lot. That's all the colours."

Gunther's nose wrinkled, as if he had just caught a whiff of milk that had been left out in the sun. "The synapses of the voters must be like lovers, reaching their moment of passion and erupting together, their erotic bounty gushing into each other – not shrivelling in a migraine of confusion!"

"I don't follow," said Dave. "Colours have meaning?"

"Associations, inferences, intimations, David Williams! Red is passion, for example, but also revolution and anger. Blue is sincere and calming, but also elitist and austere.

Yellow is cheerful, but also the colour of warning. But all these colours are taken by major parties already. So are green and purple. If you take any shade of these, you risk confusion, mistakes, distraction!"

"What about pink?" said Rufus. "The flower on our logo is pink."

"Pink is a great colour!" squawked Gunther. "It means compassion. Romance. Sensitivity. But traditionalists perceive it as weak, and progressives don't like its feminine cliché."

"Who cares what traditionalists think?" shrugged Dave.

"You do," said Riz. "If you want their vote. And you need as many as you can get."

Dave pulled out a chair and sat down. "Okay, well, what are the choices?"

Gunther pressed a button on a handset and the rainbow disappeared, replaced by just five colours and their corresponding shades.

"Behold!" He said, turning back to them with moistening eyes. "I am overcome. What a powerful moment for us, friends! Here, before you now, hiding amongst its competitors like a tiger ready to pounce, is the colour that will take you all the way to Downing Street!"

"There may be literally nothing accurate in that statement," murmured Dillon.

Riz folded his arms as he examined the screen. "Which do you think it is, Gunther?"

Gunther wiped his eyes. "Brown! You can be brown! Brown is earthy, organic, natural!"

"But it doesn't stand out," said Riz. "It's mundane."

"Then grey! It is neutral, and recessive, but also has a quiet authority. It has the scent of wisdom. Or black! Which is sophisticated and powerful. But also associated with evil, and austerity."

"I see that white is up there too," said Riz.

"Purity and innocence!" said Gunter.

Amy frowned. "Yeah, but hard to represent in white-backed media."

"It's orange," said Dillon, with a sigh. "It's clearly orange."

Gunther fell to his knees, and raised his arms in the air. "Yes! Yes, yes! It is orange! You have chosen wisely! Orange is warm, energetic, confident, offbeat! It *is* the Happening Happy Hippy Party! You have great insight, Dillon Rubin! You are orange! We are orange!"

Dillon stood up. "It's the only colour left, Gunther. Dave, today's interviews went okay in the end. We secured just under three hundred candidates. We'll do it again tomorrow and get the rest."

"Er, guys," said Amy, scrolling through her phone. "Do you normally get a lot of online hate?"

"Not really," said Catie. "We don't normally get much online anything."

Amy bit her lip. "Yeah, I think that's changing."

4

R iz bent over a laptop computer. "Hold on, I'll get the feeds up on the screen. There."

He tapped a key, and the colours on the smart-board dissolved into a dashboard of social media highlights. There was silence while the group read them.

Dillon was the first to speak. "Wow," he said. "Well, this is like putting your face in an industrial sander."

Dave's eyes were wide. "I don't think I've seen quite such an extensive juxtaposition of sex and violence since I left school."

"What school did you go to?" asked Amy.

"No, I mean – the kind of things schoolboys say."

"'Schoolboy' is right."

"Is that even biologically possible?" asked Rufus, pointing to a tweet that suggested an alternative means by which Dave could introduce a pineapple to his body.

Catie rubbed her eyes. "I doubt that scientific accuracy was the primary concern of the author," she said.

"Some of these show impressive creativity," said Dave.

"It's like Roald Dahl had an off-day and just let rip at the postman. I've never even seen half these words before."

"What's this one, here?" asked Rufus. "It sounds like a foreign city or something."

Dillon looked at him. "You don't know what that is?"

Rufus shrugged. "Is it in Turkey?"

"It's a sexual act, Rufus. With a number of participants."

"Oh! Would I – "

"Almost certainly not."

"Quite a lot of these are directed at Catie," said Dave.

"Of course they are," said Catie. "I'm the only vague minority representation in the HHHP leadership. The rest of you are three white blokes. Hell, Rufus is even an aristocrat."

"I believe it's aristo*crap*, according to this tweet, here," said Rufus.

"That's what these guys do," said Riz. "They'll zero in on anything that makes you stand out – gender, sexuality, colour, religion. It's all fair game to them."

Gunther was the door. He bowed. "I will leave you to savour this moment of great importance. The moment that the HHHP grasped its destiny, and its destiny was orange!"

"Yeah, things have moved on a bit now, thanks, Gunther," said Dillon.

"You'll get used to it, boys," said Catie. "Welcome to the club. I'll pop your membership cards in the post."

"We'll get used to it? You mean you've had this before?"

Catie shrugged. "Of course. Not on the HHHP account, on my personal feed. Sure, it's not always this nasty. Sometimes it's just, you know, mansplaining or put-downs. You try being anything other than a white, middle-class, heterosexual male online and you see what happens. Even the women are frigging horrible."

"This one's from a woman," said Rufus. "She says you have hair like Cher, Dillon."

Dillon squinted to read it. "Well, I take that as a compliment."

"This might be instigated by BEEF," said Amy. "It's all stemming from a piece on *ThinkRight*. BEEF know we're not ready, that's why they've done this. They're filling the void. We need to get something out there, urgently, or the press will start reporting on *this*."

"No," said Dave. "Why should we be bullied into rushing?"

"Because either you set the agenda, or this will. And if this does, it's not going to be 'here's an exciting new political party with the will to fight and the budget to match' but 'over-endowed amateur politicos attract online anger'. I think we need to bring the press conference forward. First thing in the morning."

"I agree," said Catie. "But Dave's never given a press conference before. He needs training."

"That's not a problem," said Amy. "I can take care of that."

"Shouldn't we respond to this?" said Dave. "I don't think we should let them fill the airwaves, bandwidth, internet-pixie-dust-whatever, unchallenged."

Rufus was tapping something out on his phone. "How about this?"

Dillon peered over his shoulder to look at it. "Bloody hell, Rufus, what goes on in your head? That's appalling. Would you let your mother see that?"

"Their mothers might quite like to," said Rufus. "You know, being in it, and all."

"No," said Catie. "You say something back and you're a cry-baby liberal, or can't cope with free speech, or your tweet gets trotted out as evidence of your own nastiness until the end of time. There's a better way. We use it to our advantage."

Dave nodded at one of the tweets. "How could this invitation to spend some quality time in the bathroom with a chainsaw possibly be to our advantage?"

She sat down, producing a notebook and pen from her pocket. "This is fantastic intelligence. What they choose to mock tells us something. It tells us what they perceive to be our weaknesses, where we're vulnerable. We use them to do our brainstorming for us. Then we plug those gaps, shore up those weaknesses."

"Catie, you don't have to do this," said Riz, as she started scrolling and scribbling.

"Are you kidding? This is the best way to fight."

"No, I mean, you've got a whole team outside. You have staff now who can do this for you."

Catie smiled, and Dave realised it was the first time he'd seen her smile for a while. In fact, he realised, he had never stopped to wonder why Catie didn't smile much.

"Oh – great," she said. "Okay well introduce me and we'll sort out a speech and some talking points for the morning, and Amy you go and teach Dave how to speak to a camera without looking like a victim in a low budget, found-footage horror movie."

AT A GOLF CLUB just outside Sandport, Alicia and Bart sat at a black-tie dinner hosted by a local dinner club. Alicia had done her best to smile and laugh politely at the conversation, but there was only so much banal chat about pensions, Hugos on gap years and sly references to fictional mistresses that she could take. It didn't help that there were, perhaps, only ten women in the room of more than a hundred and that the only people younger than fifty were serving the wine.

The club had advertised Thorne as a 'controversial speaker.' This fig-leaf was, to her mind, utterly needless. The reality was that this room, this demographic, were gasping to hear from Excelsior Thorne. And in any event, these engagements were normalising BEEF and its agenda. They could call Thorne what they liked, as far as Alicia was concerned, if they were going to let him stand up and tell jokes about asylum seekers.

After a mediocre starter, passable first course and uninteresting dessert, coffee was served and Thorne took to the podium. Alicia listened to the beginning with genuine interest – on the public stage, he was jovial, friendly and warm. He'd even written some of his own jokes. It was only in real life, she thought, that he was a complete arse.

As Thorne was explaining BEEF's plan to compel the unemployed to generate electricity on treadmills, she chose her moment to lean over to Bart.

"Bart, a word," she whispered. If you're going to dispatch your flying monkeys to deal with the HHHP, you need to run it by me first."

Bart shrugged. "I don't know what you're talking about. All I did was produce some literary art. I was caught by the whim of inspiration. I can't help being so influential," he said, and held up his fingers. "It's not my fault that these babies can play the harp of human emotion."

"Don't gaslight me, Bart. You know what we agreed in the car – I am taking care of the HHHP."

Bart smirked. "What, with your zany infiltration plan?

What are you going to do next – paint a tunnel on a wall and watch them run into it?"

"Look, don't think that just because you ghost-wrote his book that you've got some kind of special, red carpet access to Thorne. I've been in this party since it formed, Bart, and I go back further with him than you can know – I haven't just flown in from the colonies."

Bart regarded her for moment.

"Okay, Cruella, I'll bite," he said. "You know why he hired me? Because he wants to win elections. And I can do that. Look at this event. Do you think this would have happened ten years ago? Would it, hell. What were *you* getting him booked for? I'm sure everybody's very grateful that you helped to midwife the party. But, that baby's now a handsome young footballer and he's in the premiership, right? He doesn't need his menopausal mother running onto the pitch to clean his face with tissues and spit. In fact, it's embarrassing. It's grown-up time. Now shush, men are talking."

She said nothing, and Bart went back to tapping on his phone. She popped two sugar lumps into her coffee.

Alicia Rhodes had not survived this long in BEEF by losing her temper. Neither had she survived by revealing her weaknesses. Bart, however, had just shown her one of his.

Underestimation.

DAVE WILLIAMS and two a.m. had not encountered each other for several years.

Dave had assumed that it must have continued to exist, along with its neighbours, between eleven p.m. – the time he would customarily pass out in front of the television –

and nine a.m., when Ken would slam the door on his way to work. The last time that Dave had met it had been an era where it was normally accompanied by dingy nightclubs with sticky floors and cheap vodka. He had not expected to bump into it again, ten years later, in an eco-friendly office block.

Dave yawned. Dillon and Rufus had gone home some time ago, and he had just said goodnight to Amy who had left for her hotel after Dave's intensive media training. They had covered newspaper interviews, radio, television, speeches, webinars – it had been a marathon. Dave had made copious notes, but his overarching sense was that whatever it was he *wanted* to say on any given matter was precisely what he *shouldn't* say. Instead, he should keep repeating what he had been *told* to say, until something more palatable and relevant crawled up the beach of his mind.

Dave walked through the darkened office, between the cardboard boxes and discarded packing materials towards the only evidence of habitation left, Catie's office, and tapped on the glass.

"Come in," said Catie's voice.

Dave opened the door. The room was quite big, with five or six desks, colossal whiteboards on the walls, and flat-screen TVs showing news channels. Catie was sitting with her boot-clad feet up on a desk, in her familiar purple jeans and colourful baja hoodie.

Of all the party, Catie was the greatest enigma to Dave. She had certainly led a more politically engaged life than him, so far. At four years old, for example, Catie accused her playgroup of institutional sexism. This had originally been seen by the facilitators as the entertaining warblings of a toddler tomboy, perhaps one with a future in law. Catie's crayoned petition was proudly taped to the wall with the other children's incomprehensible pictures. However, after losing their appeal at the European Court of Justice, they would ultimately find Catie significantly less entertaining, and be required never to use the word 'tomboy' again.

This early incident was portentous of Catie's journey through the British education system. At six, Catie's parents received a complaint following bring-a-toy-to-school day. Catie had, according to this report, been 'corralling' the other children. Her teacher explained that she had discovered that a cuddly penguin, a plastic dinosaur and what appeared to be some kind of robot badger were participating in a needle exchange programme. The robot badger was being prescribed methadone. Meanwhile, two boys were interviewing a superhero figurine on suspicion of soliciting sex for money, while the fashion doll that was apparently the other half of the arrangement was being conveyed to a GU clinic to join six other fashion dolls waiting for appointments. Catie's teacher had been particularly upset that four of the dolls tested positive for 'clam middle-ear'.

At eight, Catie broke into the school one evening to free her class hamster, Chris. Regrettably, as Chris had been raised in captivity, he was easily apprehended and consumed by Mittens, the school cat. Mittens, of course, had resisted Catie's earlier efforts to liberate her. This did not stop Catie from bringing her own private prosecution against Mittens for Chris' death, manufacturing a little courtroom out of cardboard boxes and toilet roll tubes for the purpose.

At twelve, Catie narrowly escaped arrest for criminal damage, after her protest about her secondary school's dissection of mice was interdicted. The protest, had it gone ahead, would have resembled the final scene of the movie *Carrie*. When teachers quizzed Catie on whether she knew the difference between 'right' and 'wrong', she told them that the question was politically biased.

After university, Catie began her career in communications as a reporter for a left-wing, low-circulation magazine. After that, she became the spokesperson for a blistering range of activist organisations covering animal rights, anti-facism, arms control, biodiversity, climate change, food dumping, fracking, LGBTI rights, racism, reproductive rights, tax justice and several different kinds of poverty. Catie's CV was less like a resume than a telephone directory.

Dave had, subsequently, assumed that Catie was inherently combative; a driven woman who was evangelistic about her perspective. But, until tonight, it had not crossed Dave's mind that perhaps he really didn't know anything about Catie at all.

"Hey Dave," she said with a yawn. "You're still up. How was the media training?"

Dave waved a pad of notes. "Apparently questions don't have answers. They have 'replies'."

"Sure," she said. "Sometimes they do, though. Pull up a chair," she added, and held up her pad. "This is your speech. Help me with it."

"Okay," said Dave, sitting down. "Hit me."

She passed over a page. "This is how it signs off. See what you think."

He read it as she continued to edit the rest, and then looked up. "It's good. I mean, really good."

"No edits?" She said, without looking up.

"No, not on this page."

"Brill."

There was a pause. The only sound was that of Catie's pen as she worked.

"Catie," said Dave.

"Yep?"

"I just wanted to say, you know, after we saw all those tweets earlier – that I think it's really rough, what they were saying. And if that's the kind of thing that happens a lot, then, you know – let me know if there's anything I can do."

She looked up. "Anything you can *do*?"

"Well – yes."

Catie was quiet for a long time. After a while, a patient smile formed on her face, the kind that a parent might use with a child. She put down her pad on the desk and sat up.

"Dave," she said, leaning forward. "What is it, in particular, that you feel I may need your help with? Is it being gay, or being a woman, or being a feminist?"

"I – what?"

"Okay, look. Don't take this the wrong way. It's great that you're connecting. You've had an insight into a world, my world, that you hadn't seen before and think it looks a bit hard. Perhaps, but it isn't for me. Because it isn't about me. It's about a *lot* of people."

"I don't understand – I thought that would be a nice thing to say. You know, showing that I empathise."

"No, you're not *empathising* – you're *sympathising*."

"I'm not sure I know the difference."

"Okay, let me put it this way. Zoom out. We launch a national campaign tomorrow. But Dillon only supported it because BEEF attacked us personally. And it was only initiated by you, because some trivial, mid-morning DJ made fun of you. Rufus, meanwhile, was born with not so much a silver spoon in his mouth as a golden spatula. None of you has been spat at in the street and called a 'Paki'. None of you has had your locker at school urinated against by the football team, because you question your birth gender. None of you is assumed to know less, to be less capable, purely because of what is or isn't waving about between your legs. You three have had every opportunity that this country affords. You've been the guys that get to start the race ten seconds earlier than everyone else."

"I'm confused," replied Dave. "I'm sorry that I haven't had struggles like you – but I do care."

Catie sighed heavily and sat back. "No, not *like me*, like the people we *represent*. People whose struggles are too nuanced and complex to fit into a headline, so they get flattened by a populist steamroller, driven by media barons. Nobody expects us to experience the suffering that they do, they expect us to recognise and challenge it. Look, it's great that you've woken up. That you've had a glimpse of the reality out there. Welcome to the fight. And it is a fight, and it's one in which people are dying. Have you seen the suicide stats for LGBTI youth?"

"No – "

"Look them up online tonight. And you know, many of the people fighting against us – these people have their own pain and fears. They're just dealing with them in a catastrophically poor way. The fight is not against people, but against ideas, and the actions to which those ideas lead."

"I'm sorry," said Dave. "I guess I didn't know."

Catie shrugged. "That's one of the ways it proliferates. The space between people and between communities. The silence. So, you want to know how you can help? What you can do?"

Dave leaned forward. "What do you need?"

Catie looked directly into his eyes. "Shape up," she said, gently. "This party stops being a fringe party when you stop being a fringe leader. Learn to be a real politician, and lead this charge. You're always going on about 'doing something' – do it."

Dave swallowed. "It seems – daunting."

She gave a tired half-smile. "Yes, it is. But don't act like you're carrying the weight of the world on your shoulders, Dave. It's not all about you. You're not Luke Skywalker – you've just got a part to play. A lot of people have played parts already. And this one is yours. Whether you do it well or badly doesn't matter. Just *do* it."

Dave nodded, but was quiet for a moment.

"I've had an idea," he said. "To unveil tomorrow in the conference. How we can signal what we're all about. I was thinking about what you were saying about giving some of the money away, and about the *ThinkRight* article. I hope you'll like it."

"Oh? What is it?"

He told her, and she did.

JOURNALISTS STARTING ARRIVING NOT LONG after morning stretched across the Sandport sky. Amy had opted to hold the conference in a vegan café opposite Green House, and by eight-thirty the road was clogged with news vans and broadcast crews.

Riz was inspecting the scene from the window of Catie's office.

"What have we got, Riz?" Asked Amy, scrolling through her phone.

"Looks like a good showing," he said. "All the major TV news channels are down there. Café looks pretty full of newspaper and wire guys too. How's Dave shaping up?"

"He's showering and changing."

Riz nodded. "How was he in media training last night?"

Amy pocketed her phone. "Well, we started with a sort of rabbit-in-headlights vibe. Then we moved on to a rabbit-under-the-wheels vibe, then a sort of robot rabbit thing and called it a day when he upgraded to deer-in-headlights. We'll just have to see how he gets on."

"Morning," said Dave's voice, and they turned around. Dave stood in the doorway, wearing a charcoal-grey suit, white shirt and peach tie that a staffer had rushed out to buy. The tie brought out his pastel blue eyes, and Amy hadn't noticed those before.

She smiled. Dave looked good. She hadn't expected that.

"You still have the tags on," she said.

"Oh, right," he said, fumbling with his sleeves and collars.

"Good morning Dave," said Riz. "Did you sleep well?"

"I have no idea. I found a sofa at about three a.m. and had a nice lie-down, and the next thing I knew it was six o'clock and I was being woken up to start practicing my speech. Ask the sofa. It probably has a better recollection than me."

Amy checked her watch. "Okay, we'd better get down there. Let's walk and talk. Dave, start channelling your inner Prime Minister."

Riz handed Dave the latest version of the speech and talking points, and they left the office and began the walk down to the lobby.

"Okay, so Catie's down there now. She'll introduce you, and then invite a round of applause. That's your moment to walk over to the microphone and give the speech."

Dave nodded. "When the clapping starts, crack on."

"After you've spoken, take a couple of questions. The

questions will almost certainly be pointed, so don't let them throw you off-balance. Find a way to bring each back to our talking points."

"Right."

"And remember – this isn't an interview. You control the space. You'll only get pinned down, or backed into a corner, if you let it happen. When you're done giving your reply to a question, ask for another one and move on quickly."

"Got it."

"Let's practice now," she said, stopping them in the corridor. She turned to him and straightened his tie. "Dave, you guys are a joke party that got lucky, and now you're running around like the entitled kids of a dotcom millionaire. Why should anyone listen to anything you say?"

Dave blinked, and then rallied. "Hi, Amy, that's a great question. But I think the real issue here is, why does it take an outsider to reconnect British politics with real people? There is a crisis of trust in this country – and people need leaders who are authentic, without ulterior motives, who are who they say they are. We are exactly who we say we are."

"That's – that's actually pretty good," she said, and she meant it.

Dave grinned. "Good!"

"But don't say 'great question', though. You sound like a science teacher."

"Okay."

"And don't add to any sound-bites in the talking points, they need to be standalone lines so that the media can slot them in. Don't put 'as I've said before' at the beginning or anything like that."

They arrived in the lobby, the view of the café over the road obscured by big outside broadcast news vans with satellite dishes and generators, while uniformed police were dotted around the street.

Without warning, it had become real for Dave.

Dave's stomach seemed to twist and cavort inside him, perhaps in an attempt to make a bid for freedom through his large intestine. A hot, angry blast of terror erupted from somewhere in his chest. He reached out to an ornamental plant to steady himself.

"Dave? You okay?" asked Riz.

"Yeah," said Dave. "Yeah. Just – a couple of days ago the closest I got to broadcast news was FaceTime. And now this."

Amy nodded. "It's okay. Just focus. Focus on our key themes today – integrity, authenticity, hope."

"Integrity, authenticity, hope," repeated Dave. "Integrity, authenticity, hope."

Riz's phone rang. He answered it, and then told them: "That's Catie. It's time."

BIG SUE'S VEGAN CAFÉ had never been so full, which was ironic, because neither had her customers.

Journalists from across Britain, and several international news sources, sat patiently tapping on their phones before a crescent of video cameras and big, fluffy sound booms. The more usual floor apparatus of beanbags, tables and mismatched chairs had been banished to the back room.

The room hushed as Catie took to a microphone in front of a bright, orange HHHP banner featuring a sun rising over a countryside scene. She opened the conference by stating that they wouldn't be taking policy questions that morning, as a full manifesto would be released by the end of the week. Amy watched the reaction of the journalists present carefully, and especially when Catie finished with: "I would like to introduce David Williams, the Leader of the Happening Happy Hippy Party."

Amy helped to spark a round of applause from the party staffers present, and Dave made his way to the microphone as a fresh spatter of camera flashes illuminated the room.

"Good morning," he said. "Thank you for joining us at Big Sue's café. The banana muffins are – quite unlike anything you've ever tasted before."

"And we're off," she said to herself.

It was a good start. It wasn't Churchill, or Obama, or even Blair – but it was credible. In a way, it was even quite an impressive maiden speech for a man who, until recently, had said more to his television than he had said on it. And there was something inside Dave, some kind of spark, that flickered as he spoke. If she could turn that into a roaring fire, this insane plan might actually work.

And then, with a glance at Catie, Dave went off-script.

"As you've heard, we won't be making any policy announcements today," he said. "But there is one thing to unveil. And it is this. Politics needs more truth. Government needs more integrity. That's why we're announcing a new, non-profit organisation that will be dedicated to fact-checking the claims made by politicians on all sides during this election – including us. It will be paid for entirely by the HHHP, but as a matter of governance the HHHP will be unable to exert any influence, strategic or editorial. I am delighted then, to tell you that the Fact Checking and Knowledge Unit, the FCKU, will be launched immediately."

Amy rubbed her eyes. The FCKU. Brilliant.

"I have a little time available for some brief questions,"

said Dave. "Yes," he added, pointing to the back of the audience.

"Martha Lewandowski, *Sandport Chronicle*," said a voice. "Dave, you've been very fortunate with your endowment, which presumably reflects the strength of the donor's convictions. But what would you say to criticism that you're wasting the money, that it's naïve to fight an election campaign that you won't win?"

Dave took a sip of water. Good time-buying tactics, thought Amy. He'd been listening.

"Well," he said. "I think that kind of assumption about the electorate is exactly the sort of mistake that commentators have been making for a while. We're going to present them with a fresh take. With integrity, authenticity and hope. And we'll let them decide. Next question - yes, you."

"*Evening Post*. This morning's latest opinion poll puts the British English Emancipation Front at the top for this constituency. What's your response to that?"

"I think that's going to change dramatically when the people of Sandport see what we stand for – see what I stand for, after we publish our manifesto."

Amy nodded. Dave handled a few more questions, and Catie returned to close the conference. As she thanked everybody for coming, Amy permitted herself a smile of relief. It was a success.

"How did it go?" Whispered Dave.

"We'll debrief back at Green House," said Amy. "Just keep smiling and looking authoritative as we leave."

Amy and Dave left the café, and made their way back to the Green House lobby, Catie following behind. As the doors slid obediently to admit them, Dave turned to her.

"That journalist – she's right. And Dillon's right," he said.

"What? What about?"

"The money. This plan. It's crazy. We're going to blow the money. We should be investing in the party machine, not throwing it all away on – on this," he said, waving around him.

"It's perfectly natural to find all this a bit intimidating, Dave."

"It's not that it's intimidating," replied Dave, rubbing his temples. "It's just wrong – this isn't the right thing to do, we should be investing, not spending. A national campaign is a mistake. I need to stop it."

"No," said Amy. "Don't do that. It isn't a mistake. Listen, listen to me."

She took his hands, and moved in close, so that he had no option but to look straight into her eyes. His hands were softer, and warmer than she had expected.

"Dave, nothing about politics is the same anymore. Opinion polls are often wrong, outsider parties make ground rapidly all the time – coalitions, low-odd wins, the end of the two-party state; there's never been a better time for the HHHP to make a play."

He nodded, but said nothing.

"And you see what's going on out there. BEEF out on top, their narrative bleeding into the policies of the major parties, half the country swinging to the right and the other half to the left. The biggest electoral winner is fear. They need hope. Britain needs hope. You can be that hope."

"I suppose," he said, slowly.

She smiled. "This is the fast-track. You've put yourselves on the map in a way that a slow burn wouldn't ever do. This is the right thing, at the right time. You did great out there. It's only just beginning."

Dave nodded again.

"Okay," she said. "Come on, let's run over the itinerary."

As she led up him up the stairs back to the office, she added: "So, you didn't want to run FCKU past me?"

"AND WE'RE out of the stocks and running," said the Prime Minister, watching the end of the HHHP press conference on Starling's phone.

Starling nodded and took his phone back. "Indeed, sir."

"What a time to be alive, eh?" said the Prime Minister, removing the headphones. "Watching the television on a little piece of magic like that."

"Yes, sir."

"Ahem," said the Uruguayan ambassador.

"Oh yes, sorry," said the Prime Minister, turning back to the trade delegation waiting patiently around the conference table in a Downing Street stateroom. "Where were we? Something about soya beans, wasn't it? Here's a thought – did you know we have a band in this country called Uruguay? Isn't that remarkable!"

"Sir," whispered Starling. "I believe you may be thinking of 'Jamiroquai'."

"No, no, I'm sure it's pronounced 'Uruguay'. Are they from Uruguay? Maybe they could help with the soya beans thing."

FOR THE GREAT political parties of Britain, the formulation of policy is a long, considered and democratic process. Many have committees that consider individual ideas, producing analysis and submitting proposals. Complex, lengthy procedures ensure wide consultation with

members, local associations, parliamentarians, affiliated
organisations and even trade unions. Huge, annual confer-
ences vote to agree a fledgling programme of government.
Finally, after this exhausting process, a general election
manifesto is born into the arms of its proud party parents.

For the Happening Happy Hippy Party, however, the
formulation of party policy represented no lengthier a
process than a Friday evening in the Duck and Fiddle.

The party's economic policies had been agreed quite
early on over civilised pints of bitter. Discussion of the
bulk of its foreign trade policy had merged, with
surprising coherence, with a debate about who was
allowed to eat Catie's chips. A stalemate between Dave
and the rest of the party on nuclear weapons was broken
when Dave went to the toilet, and the party elected Jack's
dog, Spike, to stand in for him on the vote. Spike
abstained, preferring instead to investigate the floor for
fallen chips, but that was enough for the motion to carry.
Dave remembered very little of the debate about
European policy, as it had taken place during several
unwise rounds of tequila slammers and even now the
phrase 'Schengen Agreement' still made him feel a bit
green.

The HHHP's education policy, which revolved around
replacing the national curriculum with courses in things
that really mattered – such as getting away with breaking
wind in the workplace – was decided outside a kebab shop
and, of all the HHHP's manifesto, was actually adopted by a
Scandinavian country.

Rufus, who had been in charge of developing these ideas
and ultimately writing the manifesto, felt a great deal of
pride in it – but there was no way the party could run for
office on the basis of that document. Towing the country

north to off-set global warming wasn't going to stand up to public debate. And anyway, Iceland was in the way.

This was why, although the HHHP's national campaign had dominated the news cycle of the morning, the party leadership were sitting at the conference room table that afternoon surrounded by other parties' manifestos. And Rufus wasn't happy.

"Can't we have two manifestos, then?" he asked. "You know, keep this one, but write a serious one too?"

"What, a sort of 'ha ha, but no – seriously' manifesto? I think that would be the political equivalent of a Dad-joke, Rufus," said Dillon.

Rufus folded his arms. "Well, then we should just keep this one."

Dave leaned back in his chair with his hands behind his head. "We can't keep this one, Rufus – this isn't a real manifesto. It's like what you'd give a child if they asked for a manifesto to play with. This is a toy manifesto. It should be made of plastic and squeak if you squeeze it."

"Okay, I think what Dave is saying is that the joke manifesto was great when he was a none-of-the-above candidate," said Catie. "And we'll probably still capture those votes, but now we need a broader appeal."

"Yeah," said Dave. "That, and the other thing I said. That I actually said."

Catie shot him a look, and he sighed.

"Okay, look," went on Dave. "Rufus. Let's not vote on this, all right? Let's just agree that we need a new one. We'll make it up to you. This is a very funny manifesto. I love it. But Britain's not on this wavelength. We need to write something that really captures what we're about."

Rufus shrugged. "Fine. So what do you suggest, Glorious Leader?"

Amy was flicking through the other party's manifestos. "It's hard to tell the difference between BEEF's policies and some of these ones."

"Populist politics," said Catie. "All the rage, now. That's the triumph of neoliberalism. Voters have become consumers. Sell them what they think they want, whether it's good for them or not."

"Including racist and xenophobic policies," said Dillon.

"Yep," said Amy. "But reassure those who vote for them don't see themselves as racists. You know, 'I'm not racist, but –'. If they don't see the true effect of the policy, they need never question their own opinions."

"But if you have to tell people you're not racist, there's a pretty good chance that you are," said Dillon. "It's like countries that put 'Democratic Republic' in their name. If you've got to put it in the title, you're probably not one."

"But how do we challenge that?" said Dave. "How do we challenge the saviour narrative of the right?"

"By not using phrases like 'saviour narrative of the right', for a start," said Amy. "Your strength is your normality – so don't talk like you're free-styling at an open-mic socialist poetry evening in a vegan café."

Dave shrugged. "Sorry. Just trying to be, you know, leader-y."

"Where is it, Amy?" asked Rufus.

"Where's what?"

"The vegan café with the open-mic socialist poetry evening. It sounds brilliant."

"Oh. There isn't one, Rufus – I meant it as an example."

"Well, I think it's a good idea. We should do that! That could be one of our policies!"

Dillon's brow furrowed. "Rufus, I'm not sure that your own personal brand of childlike optimism is –"

"But I'm amazing at poetry! Maybe the whole manifesto could be poetry? You know, 'global warming is really alarming, support our massive programme of wind farming'."

"Wait," said Catie, suddenly animated. "That's it!"

"Rufus' rhyming manifesto?" said Dillon. "I think that it's less so."

"No, not the rhyming manifesto – Rufus! Rufus, *you're* exactly what we need. Rufus, you're the answer!"

Rufus beamed.

"What the hell was the question?" said Dillon.

"Okay, listen – everybody look at Rufus. What's the best thing about Rufus? Why do we love Rufus?"

"I'm sorry," said Dave. "I think perhaps I've misunderstood this situation. I thought we were brainstorming a new manifesto. Now I find that we are planning an open-mic socialist poetry evening and beginning some sort of team-bonding exercise."

"No," said Catie, holding up her hand. "Stick with me on this for a second, guys. Honestly, look at Rufus – what's the best thing about him?"

They paused and stared at Rufus. He sat at the end of the table, dressed in a smart, green three-piece suit, butterfly collar and bow tie. A cup of tea – china, with a saucer – was halfway to lips that sat beneath a colossal auburn moustache. Rufus would have appeared almost noble – were a sparkly, foil windmill not turning slowly in his lapel.

Dave shrugged. "He always washes up after himself?"

"He wears colourful socks?" suggested Dillon.

"It's his positivity and confidence!" said Catie. "That's why people love Rufus! And that's why they're going to love us."

"Yes," said Amy, her eyes beginning sparkle. "Catie, I think you're on to something."

"Or on something," said Dave.

"People vote for the right wing because right-wingers make them feel safe," Catie continued. "People can sleep at night, because it feels like someone is going to protect them – it doesn't matter whether the things they fear are real or not. The right-wing message is, 'hey, you're doing great, and we're going to make the bad people go away.' That's what's missing from the left – all our messaging is 'hey, look at how miserable the world is – you *are* the bad people'."

Amy was nodding. "It's true. You can't just oppose nativism, xenophobia, misogyny and any other words with high Scrabble scores. You've got to offer an alternative, something that's better, and presented in a way that's easy to connect with. Something positive, confident, and that says, 'everything's going to be okay.' You guys are all about the joy, so you're already halfway there."

Dillon's palms were pressed together, his lips resting on them. "Okay," he murmured. "Well, how about this? We're the party of love, right? So, we define that – what does that actually mean, politically?"

"I feel a bit like 'party of love' sounds like a late nineties funky house night," said Dave. "Does 'love' play well with the electorate, Amy? You almost never hear politicians talking about it. Well, mainly you hear them denying that they did the horizontal mambo with someone they shouldn't, but that's not the same thing."

Dillon shook his head. "I don't mean the fluffy sort of love, or the squelchy sort of love – I mean serious love. The kind that represents a worldview. An outward-focussed, sacrificial way of living. Where you value other people so much you are prepared to do what you need to in order to support, protect and develop them."

Catie was scribbling. "That's a speech, right there," she murmured.

"Like – love is kind, right?" went on Dillon. "So politically, maybe that means a commitment to foreign aid – and not just foreign aid that supports British interests. But aid that actually reduces poverty, whether it's in British interests or not."

"That's a great start, Dillon," said Amy. "So, what else? How else do you define love? And how else can we apply those characteristics to policy?"

"Where do you start?" replied Dillon. "Love trusts, hopes, perseveres, forgives."

"Hang on," said Rufus, leaping up and opening the door. A young man was walking past. "You! Young man! Are you one of Riz's political science students?"

The man, dark-haired in his early twenties with round, black-rimmed glasses and a sensible V-necked grey jumper, nodded. "Yes – yes I am."

"Splendid!" said Rufus, clapping his hands together. "Get in here, boy-wizard! What's your name?"

"I'm Kevin," said Kevin, nervously walking into the meeting room and looking around.

"Okay, Kevin. We want to know how we can convert the principle of forgiveness into actual policy. Go!"

Kevin, who had only been heading to the kitchen to fetch some water and now found himself the star performer in the party's policy formulation committee, swallowed. "Oh, I – um, right, I – "

"Come on, Kevin!"

"I guess – prisons?"

"Prisons?"

Catie looked up. "Go on."

"Right. Yes. So, well, prison system is basically a

medieval approach to crime, right? People do bad things, so you lock them up. But that doesn't solve the problem, it makes it worse. So, you reform the penal system, re-orientate it more to rehabilitation. See – forgiveness."

"Investing in criminals doesn't often go down well in the public space," said Amy. "Imagine outraged tabloid articles about prisons that are like holiday camps."

"But it's supported by the research," said Kevin, adjusting his glasses. "People locked up all day are going to learn something – whether it's a trade that helps them out of their previous life, or just how to do more burglaries more effectively, we get to choose."

"You did say confident and positive, Amy," said Dave. "Rehabilitation is a positive message, and we can be confident that it's a better way."

Amy smiled and shrugged. "Sure. Okay. What else have you got?"

Dave gestured to an empty seat. "Welcome on board, Kevin."

Dillon grabbed a marker, and filled a whiteboard with the characteristics that defined love. And then, over the rest of the morning, the Happening Happy Hippy Party fleshed out a manifesto that it – and more importantly, Britain – could believe in.

5

T hings moved very quickly after the launch of the manifesto and they were pushed, ready or not, into the centre of the public stage. On the day of the launch, the broadsheets went with headlines like 'New left-wing challenge', 'Hippies have high hopes' and 'Fragmenting left-wing sees new hopefuls'. The tabloids led with lower brow puns like 'Are you ready to (political) party?' and at least one went with 'Was Princess Diana a ROBOT?'

Britain's most notorious right-wing tabloid did not report on the HHHP, but that was primarily because it was two days into a week-long special on whether immigration causes cancer.

Amy's timetable was ambitious. Dave, Dillon and Rufus found themselves giving speeches at schools, parks, universities, corner shops, industrial plants, docks, hospitals, churches, recreational centres, a sixties-themed nightclub and a windmill. The latter was one of the less successful engagements, as Dave had to duck every nine seconds throughout his address. And if the speeches were not exhausting enough, in between the doorstep visits they also opened supermarkets, village fetes, several anti-fascist rallies, a hippy-themed restaurant and a sanctuary for injured newts. There were cheers at Green House when the aggregated opinion polls put the party on two percentage points, and even more so when they rose to five.

Meanwhile, the Fact Checking Unit – newly rechristened after some entertaining headlines – proved popular and industrious, challenging most of the major party's manifestos and public claims. The HHHP had been less impressed with its analysis of their own, though while it questioned some of their figures their credibility remained mostly intact. Dave Williams was most sore about the FCU's suggestion that their manifesto looked like it was written by students, not least because it was.

Before the HHHP knew it, six weeks until the election had become five, then four, then with the ruthless predictability for which time is known, three.

MARTHA LEWANDOWSKI HAD BEEN in the office since six a.m.

She found that she worked better in the mornings. Her thoughts were clearer, her productivity higher. It also meant that she could avoid the seagulls that clustered outside the *Chronicle*'s office, waiting for a momentary lapse in a visitor's concentration so that they could strafe whatever breakfast one happened to be holding. Barry, the *Chronicle*'s photographer, was a repeat victim.

Martha had finished her previous piece and moved on to a new tingle in her spidey-sense, starting by scrolling through some of the images from the HHHP's launch conference several weeks ago. There was Dave Williams, giving his speech. Whispered words between him and someone that looked a lot like Amy Cordell, previously of Downing Street. Dave's introduction by Catie Fitzgerald, previously of practically every left-wing protest movement in England. Riz Islam lurking in the wings, political gun for hire and sometime consultant to most of the major parties.

She took a sip of coffee from a cardboard takeaway cup and opened her browser. She typed 'winstanley mortimer' into an online search engine and hit return. Nothing. And no Winstanley Mortimer on the electoral roll, either. No telephone numbers listed, no social media accounts. There were a couple of registered companies linked to the name, but nothing particularly interesting about them – unless their vagueness was interesting in itself.

Her desktop phone rang, and her eyes didn't leave the screen as her hand fumbled for the receiver.

"*Chronicle*," she said.

"Martha! It's Jock!"

Martha could only just hear Jock over the sound of thumping house music, laughter and chinking glasses. She thought she heard champagne corks popping, or perhaps it was gunshots. Frankly, it could have been either.

"Hi Jock," she said to her editor-in-chief, checking her watch. "Good – er – morning. Where are you?"

"Out on a boat with some pals!" He said. "I'm wearing a captain's hat!"

A young, female, voice called someone 'baby' in the background.

"Well, um, anchors aweigh," said Martha, with a verbal shrug.

"Now, look here Martha – I've got a job for you. Have you got a pen?"

"Yep."

"There's a lady in town who's dyed her dog blue in solidarity with her voting intentions. It's a hoot. You need to get down there with Barry. We need a lovely, close-up shot of his big fluffy, face."

"Barry's?"

"No, the dog's."

"I'm kind of busy here, Jock," said Martha, glancing at the screen. "I'm looking into the big donation to the HHHP. It's weird. There's no trace of this donor anywhere. There's a story here."

There were splashes and shrieks of delight somewhere behind Jock's voice.

"Political donations?" he said. "That sounds boring, Martha! That's not what our readers want! You might as well write a leader on the sexual habits of the common slug!"

"Actually, Jock, that wouldn't be boring at all. You know slugs have penises as long as their whole bodies, right? And they glow in the dark."

"What? I can't hear you – I'm on a boat!"

"Yes, you said –"

"Great to hear you're up for this, Martha! Fluffy McFluffyface, all blue in food colouring, all cutey-cute. Off you scamper!"

With that, Jock's voice vanished, but not before announcing that it was time for 'nudey-nudey-swimmy-swimmy,' but Martha assumed that this was not directed at her.

"Come on, Barry," she said, reaching for her bag.

THE HHHP BATTLE-BUS rolled through the night.

They had managed to obtain a hybrid bus, which used both conventional propulsion and electricity, and had been stylised to look like a big Volkswagen Campervan. Catie and Rufus had originally wanted a coach powered by vegetable oil, but that would have meant being followed by an oil tanker full of the stuff – which seemed to defeat the object.

The growing army of activists at HHHP headquarters had worked out which constituencies to target most heavily. From that list, Amy had drawn up an itinerary giving the optimal sequence in which Dave and Dillon should visit them to support the local candidates. The tactic was known as a 'whistlestop tour', Amy had explained. At this particular point in the tour, Dillon's face was squashed up against the window while he snored. Catie quietly tapped away on a laptop, and Dave read the latest campaign analysis on his smartphone. Amy was away, scouting ahead, and Rufus was campaigning in London.

Dave put his phone down and looked out into the dark as they headed north. "The problem is age," he murmured. "Our support trails off beyond fifty, and then by sixty there's nobody."

Catie looked up. "Does it matter?"

"It does if we want to win any seats. We've orchestrated our whole campaign around the young vote, but we all know that older people are more likely to vote. It seems – high risk."

Catie saved her work and shut the laptop. "You're worried?"

"A little," he said, rubbing his chin.

"So you think maybe Amy's wrong? I mean, it's her strategy, right? We both influenced it, that day back in the hotel – but she totally drove that."

Dave sighed. "I don't know. She's the expert. She knows best."

Catie smirked. "Yeah."

"You don't think so?"

"Well, I don't think she has our interests at heart. I think she's motivated by what's best for her career, not what's best for the HHHP. Remember after the launch conference? I saw how passionately she persuaded you to stick with a national campaign."

"But you agreed that a national campaign was the best thing to do."

Catie shrugged. "Sure. But it's what's motivating her that makes me suspicious. And I haven't seen anything to change my mind on that. High-risk strategies – lots of glory for her if it works, and she can just go back to London if it fails. Are we just her little career experiment, Dave?"

Dave shook his head. "I've looked into her eyes. I know her. I get her. She's genuine. This is real."

Catie unscrewed a bottle of water and took a sip. "You don't think your objectivity might be – compromised?"

"What do you mean?"

"I see the way you look at her."

"Nonsense! I have no interest in her at all!"

"I see the way she looks at you."

"Really? How? What did you see? When? Was she smiling?"

Catie said nothing, and replaced the cap on her water bottle.

Dave sniffed, and then looked away. "I think we've been really lucky to get her. She's one of the best things ever to happen to this party."

Duncan Starling sat at a table in a service station, wondering what had happened to service stations.

This particular one had two different coffee shops, both playing different low-key, chill-out albums that made the foyer sound like the scene of some hipster banjo duel. Next to one was a salad bar with an entertainingly lewd name. Next to the other was a premium food retailer where you could get quail's eggs. Quail's eggs! On the motorway!

Obtaining a cup of tea had been a surprising challenge. There were seven different varieties chalked up on a board, and when he'd asked for 'English breakfast' the young gentleman behind the counter – with what Starling could only describe as an 'ornamental' beard – told him there were three different kinds of that.

He had finally ordered a 'dragonfly sunrise', and it arrived in a teapot that wasn't even one of those comfortingly bland stainless-steel ones. It was some sort of stylised far-Asian cast iron thing. It looked like it would be less at home on the M6 than refreshing negotiators during the surrender of an island somewhere in the South China Sea. And it wasn't like this sort of nonsense was limited to Britain. He'd been in a German one, once, with a men's room so clean and futuristic that he almost washed his hands in a urinal.

Starling could remember when service stations were service stations. A cup of tea and a greasy plate of egg and chips were priced somewhere between a month's salary and your first-born, and the only tea variation available was milk in, or out. If you asked for as much as a slice of lemon they'd look at you as if you'd politely asked whether anybody would mind if you twiddled your nipples to pick up alien broadcasts.

Starling poured some tea into a little china cup. The gentrification of service stations. What next? Artisan bus stops?

"Hi, Duncan," said a familiar voice, and he looked up to see Amy sit down at the table.

Starling glanced around. "Were you followed?"

"Followed?" said Amy. "I'm a press officer, Duncan, not Jason Bourne."

"Well, we've got to be – you know, careful. Do you have a cover story?"

"Cover story? Have you gone wrong?"

"What if we're spotted?"

"I think we can take the risk, Q. How are you? How are things back at the haunted castle?"

Starling poured some milk into the tea from a blue and white jug. "Same old, same old. The PM is getting frazzled. He did at this point in the last election campaign too."

"Are you using your sorcery to keep the hacks from looking too far into Winstanley Mortimer?"

Starling shrugged. "There's so much going on these days that it's a lot easier than I expected. They can't keep up with everything. But more importantly, I read your manifesto."

He tapped his finger on a copy sitting on the table. "It's very good. There are things in here we should be considering at the next party conference."

"Well, I think so," said Amy.

"I can't put my finger on what it is," said Starling, his brow furrowed in thought. "Maybe it's 'hope'. Optimism. It sort of says to the reader, 'I get you, and it's going to be okay'."

Amy nodded. "That's what we were going for."

Starling stirred his team. "Well, you hit it. So, tell me more about the campaign. What's the strategy?"

"All right. We're investing heavily in social media. The aim is to galvanise young people in particular, and get them out on the streets. You know, cultivate a revolutionary vibe.

We'll direct that energy across all constituencies through a single, coherent campaign plan based around face-to-face contact."

"So, it's a doorstep campaign?"

"Yes – but we're also spending a lot on digital. Using big data to target individuals with specific, relevant messages, and creating high production-value viral campaigns."

Starling tapped his spoon on the side of the teacup and placed it on the saucer. "And in terms of those messages – I haven't heard you attack the government yet, Amy. Is that wise? Shouldn't you be on the offensive?"

Amy shook her head. "They don't want a negative campaign, they don't want to throw mud because they think that's one of the things that homogenises politicians in the minds of the electorate. Instead, they're putting their energy into selling their ideas through narrative. You know, stories – that connect."

Starling sipped the tea. It was rather good, actually. "Sounds like you're going after the young vote. That's brave," he added, replacing the cup on the saucer.

Amy shrugged. "Major parties write them off because they're less likely to vote, but you know – you have to understand why that is."

"Well, I think we know why that is Amy – they don't see politics as relevant, they don't think it impacts upon their interests."

"That's certainly the Westminster narrative. But go deeper. Take Millennials. The economic trends that benefitted their parents harm them. They have crippling debt, live in an intense social-media fuelled spotlight – why should they think an established party would change their lives? Is it any wonder they don't trust politicians or see elected office as honourable? What's missing is hope,

Duncan. That's why the HHHP is ideal – it's a new vehicle. Their vehicle. As long as the HHHP speaks their language, we could tap that well of energy."

Starling raised an eyebrow. He was quiet for a moment, and the smiled. "It's great to see you this energised, Amy. I haven't for a while. And Dave Williams? How is he doing?"

"Dave is coming along nicely," she said, but he caught her involuntary smile.

Starling sat back. "It sounds like you rather like them, Amy."

Amy shook her head. "Sure, I like the *idea* of them – they're a fresh take. They're in nobody's debt, they have no hidden interests, they have a totally new message. But like them? Are you kidding? They're like children lost in a supermarket."

"Not quite in *nobody's* debt," said Starling. "You're not going native on us, Amy, are you?"

Amy reached over and drew Starling's cup and saucer towards her. She sniffed the tea. "You know me, Duncan. I'm a professional. I've got a job to do, and I'll do it. What sort of tea is this?"

Starling shrugged. "Something to do with insects, I think."

"I might get one," she said, looking up at the counter, where the beard was using the human attached to it to serve an elderly lady. "Want anything?"

Starling shook his head, and watched her carefully as she strode over to the counter.

It was first light as the HHHP battle-bus growled into the northern coastal town of Seahaven, its headlamps piercing through the morning mist that hung over rolling hills and a thousand shades of green. It bumped down cobbled streets, weaving between stone cottages and thatched roofs as it descended into the town centre.

The bus pulled up outside the local campaign head-quarters, an old fish and chip shop that had been painted such a vivid shade of orange that it might have been visible from space. Dave and Dillon stepped out into the cold morning damp, and a man and a woman scurried out of the building to greet them. The sound of seagulls and clinking boat equipment drifted over from the small harbour nearby.

"Hello, hello," gushed the woman, tubby and energetic in a bright pink waterproof. "I'm Sylvia, Michael's election agent. What a pleasure to meet you both! And aren't you so young? How lovely!"

"Er, hi," said Dillon, bending slightly to shake her hand. "I'm Dillon, and this is Dave."

Sylvia beamed. "Dave, how super-duper. Let me introduce you to Michael!"

Michael nodded. While Sylvia was small and endowed with the energy of a puppy encountering a vacuum cleaner, Michael was almost as tall as Dillon and exuded serenity. Long, tangled grey hair curled down his shoulders and sparkling eyes sat behind crimson-rimmed spectacles. He smiled, and held out his hand.

"David," he said. "Lovely to meet you. Dillon, good to see you again."

"Now," said Sylvia, holding up a clipboard. "There's a lot to do today and I'd better get over to the parish centre to oversee preparations for the meet! Oh, you must be Catie," she added, ticking her notes as Catie emerged from the bus behind them.

"Good morning," said Catie, rubbing her eyes.

"Why don't you come with me to the parish centre," said Sylvia, grabbing Catie's hand and leading her away. "We'll leave the boys to their political chat!"

Dave braced inwardly, but Catie just mumbled agreement. She looked too tired to kill anybody just now, anyway.

"Dave," Catie called out as she walked away. "Don't forget – we need to be on the road by lunchtime to have you in London for the Paxton interview tonight."

"Are you hungry?" Asked Michael. "Why don't you come inside for some breakfast?"

Michael led them both into the chip shop, which was now plastered with party posters. The shop-front area still smelled strongly of batter. In fact, thought Dave, it smelled strongly of *fresh* batter.

"We inherited a deep fat fryer when we leased the building," said Michael. "We've been experimenting with it. Have you tried deep-fried chocolate bars?"

Dave shook his head as Michael led them into the back, through a barren kitchen area, to a small room with a low table and a few chairs. A kettle was boiling on an electric stove, and a window looked out on a small garden. A dusty old radio played classical music.

"Sit down, chaps," said Michael, as he hacked a few slices of bread from a loaf sitting on the side.

"Great place you have here, Michael," said Dillon. "Interesting choice, though."

Michael laughed softly as he popped the bread into a toaster. "We went for location," he explained. "We're right in the centre here."

"And you inherited the garden, as well," said Dave, looking out of the window. "It's rather lovely out there."

The kettle whistled, and Michael poured it into a waiting china teapot. "Well, we did that – it was an overgrown mess when we arrived. All brambles. But I think we should leave things tidier than we found them, don't you, David?"

Dave nodded. "I do. So, Michael, congratulations on becoming the party's candidate for Seahaven. How did you find us?"

Michael plated up the toast, and with Dillon's help brought it and the teapot to the table, where several mugs were waiting with a jug of milk and pots of jam.

"Well, actually David, I've been in the party for years. At least, I think I have been, anyway. I've sent off an application form a few times. I tried to donate too, but your website doesn't seem to work."

"Yeah, we've had, er, some problems with organisation."

"That's okay. Maybe there's a reason you've been asleep until now. There's a great evil rising from its slumber, all over the world, you know. Perhaps it's right that this is the moment for great heroes to wake up too. As long as you don't just roll over and go back to sleep. Tea?"

"Yes, please. So, what attracts you to the party?"

Michael poured the steaming tea into the mugs, and gestured to the jams. "Please, dig in. The jams are all local. Sylvia makes them. That one's plum, that one's blackberry, I think. I haven't the faintest idea what this murky one is – maybe figs or something. Not that I've ever seen a fig growing round here."

"Thank you," said Dave, reaching for the mystery jam.

"What attracted me, hm. Well, I suppose, it's been a very long time since I found a party that seemed to connect with the values of those years. They seem so long ago. But I never gave up hope that what we all wanted, what we knew was right, could one day become part of the mainstream."

Dave paused, toast halfway to his mouth. "You mean – you were a hippy?"

Michael smiled. "Of course! Aren't you? I mean, you can't have been there, obviously – you're all far too young. But this *is* the Happening Happy Hippy Party, is it not?"

"Well yes, it is, I just –"

"Haven't met a real hippy before?" Michael winked, and took a bite of toast.

Dave glanced at Dillon, who shrugged.

"Well – no," he admitted.

"That's all right," said Michael. "You probably have, actually. And I think that's what's so exciting. That's why my heart feels like it's beating again now."

Dillon sipped his tea. "I don't follow."

Michael munched on his toast for a moment. "All right, listen. Being a hippy, it was a movement, you see. There was the music, and the pot of course, and all that fluffy stuff about love. But what the normals couldn't understand at the time was that there was something deep underneath it. A spirit, if you like – a force that drove it, into which we all connected. A sense of agreed values. It was strong."

Dave and Dillon both nodded.

"That's why anything seemed possible," went on Michael. "We thought we could change the world because that sense of harmony was so intense. But, of course, you need more than 'spirit' to live on. And, as with all things, there was a darkness. People got sick, the drugs took their toll, people drifted away. Got on with their lives. Some sold out completely of course, arriving in the Eighties with hangovers and rehabilitating themselves into grey suits and jobs in the City."

Michael took a sip of tea and paused again.

"But I took those values, that spirit, with me. And I've

waited ever since for something serious in politics that connected with it. That deserved its blessing. Until you guys. And this is the thing – I think everybody else did too. Even those in the suits. They carry it too, deep down. David, I think we can win them back. I think we are winning them back."

"We've been targeting the young vote," said Dillon. "It sounds like you think there might be a sizeable senior vote too."

Michael nodded. "Of course. That's what I'd tell those damn pollsters that keep ringing, if I actually wanted to speak to them."

"Hang on," said Dave. "You don't participate in opinion polls?"

"Why should I take ten minutes out of my life to help a corporation? I don't know anyone that does. And the samples are self-selecting. You've got to be the kind of person who likes participating and tells the truth when you do."

Michael smiled mischievously. "And I'm neither," he added.

Dave and Dillon glanced at each other.

Dillon turned back to Michael. "If you don't mind me asking, Michael – how old are you?"

Michael laughed. "I'm seventy-one. Now, have you finished? Shall we pop over to the parish hall? I suspect Sylvia might have a coronary if we're late."

"Yes," beamed Dave with renewed energy. "Let's do this!"

EXCELSIOR THORNE STOOD at the bar of the Boatman's Arms, guffawing heartily with the patrons, a pint pot of bitter in

one hand and the other slapping someone on the back. Bart
and Alicia sat at a table, Bart with a national newspaper and
Alicia pouring coffee into a cup. She watched Thorne while
she waited for Bart to finish reading. He was at his best -
everybody's friend. It was impossible to tell how blindly
angry he really was.

Bart put the newspaper down.

"Damn it," he said. "Our lead in the polls is wafer-thin
and we didn't need this right now. We need a response. We
need to do something. Something to soften his image."

Alicia didn't look up from her coffee. "There's an otter
sanctuary up the road. I think a walk-around there might do
him the world of good. Lots of pictures of Thorne with children, cuddling otters – a nice set of 'family man' photo ops."

Bart nodded. "That's good. That's a really good idea."

Thorne finished shaking hands with one of the other
drinkers and made his way over to their table. As he walked,
his face transformed from sparkling joviality to dark fury.

"Well," he said, sitting down and holding up Bart's newspaper. "What are you going to do about this fetid pile of
arse, then?"

He jabbed his finger against the offending article. It
wasn't the only one. The FCU had completed a comprehensive debunk of BEEF's manifesto, from its claims about
immigration, to capital punishment, to taxation, and every
newspaper in Britain had its own unwelcome headline to
report the matter. Alicia suspected that this one – 'Execu-
tions and exclusivism: Excelsior Thorne's medieval Britain'
– particularly annoyed Thorne, as he had always thought
that medieval Britain sounded like quite an attractive place.

She opened her mouth to speak, but Bart was in full
flow before she had even selected her words.

"I think you need to soften your image, sir," he said.

"And there's an otter sanctuary up the road. I think we should get you out there, surrounded by families, showing what a great fellow you are. You could do a speech about family values."

It was amazing, thought Alicia. He didn't even glance at her. A quite remarkable human being.

"Yes," said Thorne. "Yes, I like that. And the HHHP? What are they doing?"

"They're focussed on a national campaign right now," said Bart. "That means that Williams is hardly around this constituency. Which is fine for us. We're still leading."

"Okay, good. Alicia - make Bart's idea happen."

"Yes. Of course," said Alicia, and popped two sugar lumps into her coffee.

DAVE WILLIAMS HAD NEVER FELT SO alive, and was starting to feel a rather odd new feeling about the people he had met today. He suspected that it might be 'respect'.

The crowds throbbed through the streets of Seahaven, cheering, clapping and chanting. Orange 'VOTE HHHP' placards bobbed around on top of the throng, and the bewildered local police struggled to hold back the well-wishers.

It was Michael, thought Dave, as he approached the battle bus. He had been fascinating to watch at the husting. He spoke gently, but with an infectious confidence, and made the values he described come to life. It was like listening to a master storyteller, but the story he told was about the future – and it was everybody's future, and it sounded like a brilliant place to be.

Dave turned to him and shook his hand. "This has been

a fantastic morning, Michael," he said. "Thank you. You were amazing. I learned so much."

Michael smiled. "It's over to you from here on in, David. Remember – the world needs great heroes now. Don't roll over and go back to sleep."

Dillon climbed up into the bus, and Dave gave a final wave to the crowd, before following him.

Dave looked up to find Catie standing in the aisle. Her expression was enough for him to inwardly brace.

"We're very late," she said. "And we're only going to get later with all these crowds in the streets."

"Relax," said Dillon, flopping into a seat. "The cops are going to give us an escort."

The doors hissed shut and Catie tapped the back of the driver's chair.

"Yes, well, I expect that all that means is we have a slightly more flishy-flashy four-hour crawl to the motorway. Come on, let's go!"

"I bet a police escort's right up your street, right Dave?" smiled Dillon.

Dave shrugged. "You know, if you'd said that a couple of weeks ago, I'd have agreed," he said. "But it doesn't seem, sort of, important anymore."

Dillon cocked his head to one side. "Well, well – did the people of Seahaven get to you, Mr Williams?"

"They really believe, Dillon. Listen to them. They really believe in us."

Catie scowled. "Yes, well, it's very heart-warming that you're having an epiphany about the honour of the noble office entrusted to you Dave, but if you're late for the Anthony Paxton interview tonight and we have to send, I don't know, a cat or something, then your people's love for the Glorious Leader might take a hit. Oh, for goodness sake! It won't stop!"

Catie howled as her phone rang, and she answered it on loudspeaker without even checking the screen. "Yes, Catie Fitzgerald, come on then. I'm very busy and annoyed."

"Oh, er, hi Catie – this is Martha from the *Sandport Chronicle*."

"Martha, hi, lovely to hear from you, et cetera. What can I do for you?"

"Well, look, I've just got a few questions about the HHHP's funding, actually."

Catie slumped into a seat with a thud. "Go on."

"Was Winstanley Mortimer an active member of the party, prior to that donation?"

"No, we don't have a record of his party activity, Martha."

"But you have a record of his membership, right? An application form, a line on a spreadsheet, right?"

Dillon pointed to Catie's phone and drew his finger across his throat. "Kill this call," he whispered. "This isn't going to end well."

Catie waved him off. "I don't have that to hand," she said. "We're on the road right now. But I'll make some enquiries at HQ and get back to you."

"You see, I've done some digging into Mr Mortimer, Catie, and what's really striking about someone that makes such a generous donation is his lack of footprints. I mean, he's like a ghost. There's some companies in Africa, it seems – but also some connections to opaque organisations and accounts in the Cayman Islands. How do you feel about a donor with those sorts of connections?"

"Martha, you and I both know we can't vet every donor –"

"Sure, but this isn't just any donor, is it? It's not old Mrs

O'Leary and her ten pounds a month subscription. Can I ask what due diligence you carried out?"

"Okay, it sounds like we need to be quite transparent here. Can you send me a list of your questions? You've got my e-mail. We'll go through each issue and comment. Would that work?"

"Yes, that –"

"Great, bye Martha."

Catie jabbed her screen to turn off the phone and threw it on the table.

"Bloody hell," said Dillon.

"Hell, Dillon, will be me if we don't get to London in time," she snapped, turning to the driver. "Pedal faster!"

MARTHA LEWANDOWSKI HAD LEARNED to trust her instinct a long time ago. It was a strange sort of cerebral tingle, a quiet effervescence at the back of her mind. She had first felt it while writing for her university's student newspaper, years ago. It had resulted in an article, which, amongst the usual poorly constructed and spell-checked waffle, was a genuine expose into the links between the medical school and a pharmaceutical firm. That piece had inspired her to give up her medicine degree and go into journalism. Well, that and being asked to leave the medical school.

She sat cross-legged on the living room floor of her tiny flat, surrounded by print-outs, photos and hand-scrawled spider charts. A cold, half-eaten pizza sat in its box, staring miserably at a nearly-empty bottle of wine that had received much more attention. The news silently flickered to itself on the television.

She wasn't sure that it was money laundering, because

she couldn't see how the circle completed itself. Neither was she convinced of corruption either, as the HHHP lacked the power to make good on shady promises. So, what was it? Whatever it was, her whole brain was tingling.

Martha's phone rang, and she reached for it without leaving her thoughts.

"*Chronicle*," she said, distantly.

"Martha! It's Jock!"

"Jock, hi," she said, leaping up. "Jock I'm glad it's you, we need to talk."

Jock's voice sounded distant against the garbled rush of wind, and a thundering noise that sounded like helicopter rotors or heavy rain.

"We certainly do!" he said. "There's a big story afoot!"

Martha was surprised. "Well, yes, there is," she said. "How did you know? And where are you?"

"I'm fox hunting, Martha! With some pals from the city! Bloody good fun! I nearly caught the bugger too, you know – gave him a good whack with my stick before he got away. Went under my horse, clever! Crafty bastard!"

Martha was pacing. "But – isn't it illegal to hunt foxes?"

"Is it? I haven't the faintest idea. We don't hunt a regular fox of course because you get those bloody little protesters. No, we use a stand-in fox."

"A stand-in fox?"

"That's right. Some chap from the village. We chase him and then throw him a few quid for it. Sometimes the dogs get there first, of course. They're quite slavering, you know! Bitey!"

Martha rubbed her temple with her free hand. "Okay, that's – wow. Jock, we need to talk about this story. Winstanley Mortimer, the big donor to the HHHP. I just got off the phone with Catie Fitzgerald, their comms person, and she basically admitted that he wasn't active in the party. And they were evasive about whether he was even a member, and wouldn't say what due diligence they'd done. There's something going on here, Jock."

"What on earth are you talking about?" said Jock as a horn sounded somewhere in the background. "No, no, I'm talking about the big story! This big threat to dogs – dyeing their fur for political reasons. It's an epidemic, Martha. It's everywhere! The latest fatuous fashion fad killing our nation's beloved pets!"

"The dog-dyeing? That's what you're talking about? But – we wrote a cutesy article about it, we helped to fuel that –"

The barking was getting louder, and someone was shouting for help. "What? I didn't hear that Martha! Anyway, big expose, lots of pictures of depressed looking dogs and odious owners with fags hanging out of their mouths! Find a scientist somewhere to say it's giving the dogs haemophilia or something!"

"That's a genetic condition, Jock, you don't –"

"Brilliant! I see the headline now – 'DYEING TO DIE'. Something like that maybe. Anyway, glad you're on board. Got to go, I think the fox is hiding in a public toilet. Tally-ho!"

THE M6 WAS AT A STANDSTILL.

Not that this was particularly unusual for the M6 itself, of course, but it was certainly a matter of great chagrin for the twenty-three miles of stationary traffic sitting patiently on it – and for the HHHP battle-bus, standing like a vividly-coloured island in a sea of sensible saloons and hatchbacks.

Catie had held out hope of making the Anthony Paxton

interview even as they left Seahaven late, and even still as they left a service station where they collected Amy. But that was two hours ago – and they could still see the service station behind them.

"Well," she sighed, staring at her phone. "The good news is that our polling just hit ten per cent. The bad news is we're not going to be able to capitalise on that by having Dave on Anthony Paxton tonight."

"It's okay," murmured Amy, without looking up from her phone. "I've sent Rufus."

There was a pause, and everybody looked at Amy.

"What?" she said. "Why can't Rufus do it? The only other people we've got in London tonight are the local parliamentary candidates and none of them have the profile for it. Well, apart from the one who was on that show where members of the public pitch their inventions to angry, rich people. But the invention was some kind of gymnastic sex contraption, so I didn't think it was a good idea."

The silence went on for a moment longer, and then Dave was the first to speak.

"Rufus is great," he said. "But I'm not sure that we are best represented by a man who dresses and behaves like a nineteenth-century gentleman adventurer who's fallen through a time tunnel and woken up in a wondrous age of flying machines and beepy-screens."

"I disagree," replied Amy. "I don't think you have an option. You can't cancel or they'll never have you back. And you can't put up a nobody. Rufus is the lesser of two evils. And he might surprise you."

"On *Paxton*?" Replied Catie. "The monster that baby MPs get warned about if they don't do their homework?"

Dillon was smiling. "I think it might be rather fun."

"Dillon, no," said Dave. "Amy, you have to reverse this. We can do a live link from the bus or something."

"It's too late. He'll be in the studio by now."

"Did you see what he did to that junior minister? He basically unpacked her. Not her argument, *her*. It was like she was dissected on the table. He practically offered a bit to his dog."

"She did that to herself, Dave," replied Amy. "She didn't have the answers. Rufus will be fine – he doesn't have to set the world on fire, he just has to be there, and be genuine."

"Yes, well," said Dave, sitting back in his seat and looking at the parade of cars outside. "I think that a consequence of putting Rufus on might be that there actually is a fire."

DUNCAN STARLING SAT behind the wheel of his BMW, staring at the car in front. Neither of them had moved in half an hour, and even then, that last movement had only been three feet. He should have headed back to London last night, not mess about with meetings. This was it, he thought. His penance. He was supping with the devil, and now he was going to have sit here for hours with nothing to do but think about what he had done.

Maybe it was his mother that sparked his political career. She had been so keen on justice, had taught Starling to make his life count. Perhaps that's what set him off – a hope that he could make the world better. That he could contribute in her memory. He thought she'd have been so proud when they reached Downing Street. And is this what that political career had come to, now? Riding sidecar to the Prime Minister doing wheelies all over ethics, the law, the sanctity of democracy?

He didn't care what Amy had said about just doing her job. He knew Amy. They – those hippies – were getting inside her head. They were reaching her. She was becoming part of their imagined revolution. And the worst thing was that he actually envied her. He remembered that feeling, of possibility – of hope and *being* the hope. That the world doesn't have to be a basket case – it can be changed. It can be helped. He had lost that feeling a long time ago, suffocated in the maelstrom of Westminster life.

He had wanted to follow Amy up onto that battle-bus. He could actually see the damn thing in the rear-view mirror, looming accusatively over the cars. A big, vengeful orange cenotaph in memory of Duncan Starling's integrity.

No. He needed to take his mind off this, silence his conscience. He picked up his phone and began live-streaming the evening political show hosted by Anthony Paxton.

THE ORDERED SILENCE of the banqueting hall was almost claustrophobic as the Queen delivered her after-dinner speech. Neither the guests nor the staff wanted to be the source of any distraction, not *here*, and so they sat in regimented stillness with eyes as fixed as those of her foot guards outside.

She concluded with a gentle, but witty, aphorism – and the silence was gone in an instant, overwhelmed by enthusiastic laughter that evolved into healthy applause. With an understated smile, the Queen descended back into her seat, removed her thin-rimmed reading glasses and placed her cue cards on the table. A white-gloved attendant flicked off a discreet microphone.

"An excellent speech, your Majesty," said Dave, at her right-hand side.

"Thank you, Mr Williams," she replied, permitting herself a slight blush. "I am grateful for your counsel about the final line. I had my reservations – I have your wit to thank."

Her perfume, the delicate scent of carnations and jasmine, had returned to her seat with her.

Dave smiled. "Don't mention it, your Majesty."

For a moment, a shade crossed the Queen's face – as if she was about to add something, something important, and she glanced up to meet Dave's eyes. But as quickly as it came, it vanished, and she looked away.

There was a pause.

"David," she said, softly. "One's friends have been known to call one 'Lilibet'."

"Dave, Dave wake up – it's starting."

Blearily, Dave opened his eyes. Buckingham Palace was gone – and Anthony Paxton was on the screen of the battle-bus TV, the greying hair and wrinkling skin of a career under studio lights atop a sensible suit and tie.

"I think he's finishing the previous item," said Amy, pointing a remote control at the screen and turning up the volume.

"But questions are intensifying for British defence companies about the ethics, and in some cases the legality, of their behaviour in Africa. The Prime Minister today promised greater resolve, and most robust responses, around any arising allegations. Now, on to the election campaign. It has been a turbulent one, and one with plenty of surprises so far."

"It's on! Dillon!" Called out Catie, and Dillon appeared from further down the bus.

"Ah," he said, rubbing his hands together. "Brilliant."

"One of those surprises has been the last-minute rise of the Happening Happy Hippy Party," said Paxton. "Their manifesto draws on ideas from across the left and centre, and despite an absence of parliamentary experience, the party is currently polling at between ten and twelve per cent. Depending on the talking-head, this either relates to a cross-spectrum appeal, or to a well-financed campaign stemming from a generous single donor. With me is Rufus Lane-Seymour, the party's treasurer and finance spokesman."

Rufus filled the screen. He was wearing a white, three-piece suit with a lilac tie and matching carnation in his lapel. His face was one of comprehensive, wide-eyed terror.

"What's he wearing?" asked Dave. "Has he been to a wedding?"

"Rufus," went on Paxton. "Have you bought your party's popularity?"

The Adam's apple in Rufus' throat bobbed as he swallowed hard.

"I – I don't know how we would do that, is that – is that an option?"

Dillon smiled. "And it begins," he said, putting his feet up on the table.

"Is that 'an option'?" repeated Paxton. "This is a reasonable question, and satirising it isn't going to get you very far, is it? Do you think your popularity is a function of how much you've spent?"

Rufus was shaking his head like a schoolboy in the headmaster's office. "No, no, people like us because we've got good policies. We're new, you see. They – they want something new."

Paxton shuffled some papers. "Policies, yes, I've been

looking at those. You say you would abolish tuition fees, for example; a blunt attempt to harvest younger voters, I suspect. But it will come at some expense, and there is evidence that abolishing tuition fees doesn't do much to narrow the gap between rich and poor students. Is your policy just about winning the election?"

"This is like watching a curious gorilla dismembering a child's doll," said Dillon.

"Shh," said Amy.

"Well, no I think if you – you know, look at the sums, you can see that it will work as part of our, you know, wider, er, thing."

"The sums, yes, let's talk about those – the FCU, a non-profit organisation that *you* fund, thinks that they don't stack up, Rufus. What do you have to say about that?"

"Well, I don't have them to hand I'm afraid, so, well, nothing. Would you like a wine gum?"

"I – what? No, no thank you."

Paxton was caught visibly off-guard as Rufus produced a small white bag of sweets and popped a couple in his mouth, but he rallied quickly. "So, with every student in the country enjoying free tertiary education, what would you do about the SLC?"

"Well," mumbled Rufus with his mouth full of wine gums. "I think the risk can probably be reduced with proper sex education in schools."

"Rufus, can you not –"

"Oh!" said Rufus. "I'm terribly sorry, how rude of me."

"Thank you –"

"Would any of you like one?"

Rufus' image on the screen became hazy and ill focussed as he got up and offered the bag around to the camera crew. Anthony Paxton looked on in disbelief.

"This – in the history of this programme, this hasn't happened before," he said, as Rufus returned to his seat.

"You know, you're always very grumpy, Mr Paxton," said Rufus, selecting another sweet. "It's probably because people are always lying to you. Do you know what I do when I get grumpy? I have a sweetie."

Rufus reached over and offered the bag to him again.

"No, I don't want one, and I want you to start answering my questions."

"But I am," said Rufus. "I don't know the answer to some of them, so I'm not going to pretend that I do. And I think that's what makes us different, you know. Pink shrimp?"

"No."

"The thing is, everybody's had enough of professional politicians and their sound-bites. People like us because we're getting out on the doorsteps and having a lovely cup of tea with them. Pontefract cake?"

"No, Rufus."

Rufus grimaced, inspecting it. "No, me neither," he said, replacing it in the bag. "You see, you can't fit the entire debate on education and its place in the social and economic picture of this country into a five-minute interview, however confrontational. So, we take the time to talk to people about what we think we might do, and see whether they like it. You should come out with us. It'll be fun."

"Bloody hell," said Dave. "He's nailed it. He's only bloody nailed it!"

"Go Rufus!" cheered Catie, clapping.

Dillon beamed. "Good lad," he said.

"Now," Rufus went on. "I was talking to one of our local parliamentary candidates earlier today, and he was telling me about a fantastic invention that he's developed."

"Oh no," said Amy. "Oh no, stop him – stop him!"

6

It was hot even now, in the darkness, in the small Kundungan town. Not the raw, angry heat of the north that scorched everything in its path. This was an all-pervading humidity, that settled imperiously over the low houses and made breathing feel like inhaling hot tea. It sedated the barks of the dogs, deafened the laughing, drunken cries of the men in the streets, and had brought Callaghan out in a copious sweat the moment he stepped out of the hotel.

He sat at a plastic table in a ramshackle, open-air bar. All the bars here were the same; holes-in-the-wall through which drinks were produced from old ice-boxes, to be consumed under dusty canopies on mismatched patio furniture. His shirt, clean that day, was now sodden. He took a glug of the local Star beer, grateful for this sliver of cool.

His drinking partner sipped water from a plastic bottle, and seemed in no such discomfort. His broad, white smile beamed atop a smart suit, dry and neatly pressed.

"Mr Obi and Mr Uba want their money back," he said.

Callaghan replaced the beer on the table. This surprised

and alarmed him, but he maintained his composure. With individuals like his companion, one only shows that which it is advantageous to show.

"But we have an agreement, Mr Okoro," he said.

"We had an agreement. It has been compromised."

"This is the first I've heard of such a thing," said Callaghan. "Come, Mr Okoro – tell me your concerns. I am sure there is no need to worry."

Mr Okoro unbuttoned his pristine suit, showing – to Callaghan's further surprise – a waistcoat underneath, and drew a folded piece of paper from an inside pocket. He placed it on the table.

Callaghan reached into a crumpled jacket lying over the back of his chair, collected his spectacles and inspected the paper. It was a print-off from an internet news site, carrying the headline 'Skywolf missile: NCA investigates BDE'.

"I don't understand," said Callaghan, pushing the paper back towards Mr Okoro. "This is an investigation into British Defence Enterprises. That's a completely different company. A competitor. They have nothing to do with our deal. And even this investigation won't come to anything – it's just a delay. A routine, environmental risk."

"Mr Obi and Mr Uba are not happy. In this part of Africa, a government shows leadership. It guides its police and its press. Mr Obi and Mr Uba feel that this demonstrates that your government is unable to control its own executors. You are – unreliable."

Mr Okoro leaned in so closely that Callaghan could smell the jollof rice on his breath. "Mr Obi and Mr Uba do not like to deal with the unreliable."

Callaghan shrugged and removed his glasses. "I'm sorry, Mr Okoro, but there is no breach of our agreement and I don't recognise your concerns. The transaction has already been made. Our agreement stands."

Mr Okoro shook his head. "It does not. The agreement is void. And we will reclaim the funds."

"No deal, Okoro."

Mr Okoro took a sip of water and let Callaghan wait for his reply. "We know where the funds are, and we will take them back."

"Oh?"

He laughed. "You are not the only ones with friends all over West Africa! The funds were in the account of a 'David Williams' before they left Kundunga, and we will find him with ease. Perhaps, Mr Callaghan, you will be more willing to co-operate now that I have told you this?"

Callaghan downed the last of the beer, and stood. "I have no idea whether that's true, Okoro. All I know is that the money isn't in Africa anymore, and the agreement stands. See you next time. Thanks for the beer."

He pulled his jacket on as he walked away, and did not hear Mr Okoro raise a mobile phone to his ear and state: "This is Okoro. Get me the Panther."

A CLIP of Rufus offering a bag of sweets to Anthony Paxton's film crew was the week's second biggest social media trend. The biggest was the subsequent clip of Rufus explaining an acrobatic sex machine to Paxton himself. But Rufus' natural charm, and some strong answers that seemed to challenge the very nature of British political discourse, had done the trick.

The broadsheets covered the HHHP's ratings bump with leaders like 'Hippies rise in polls', 'HHHP sweeten Paxton' and 'Hippies high again', a theme echoed by a tabloid's 'How high can the hippies get?' Another headlined with 'Did Churchill know about ALIENS?'

Britain's most notorious right-wing tabloid did not report on the HHHP, as it was busy being outraged about a famous actress's highly revealing dress and had needed five full pages to print all the relevant photographic evidence.

The HHHP Battle Bus finally rolled into London at four am that morning. Blearily, they disembarked, and gratefully ambled into the soft lighting of their central London hotel.

Dave, lost in a fantasy of Egyptian cotton sheets, espresso machines and lots of sleep, almost walked past Rufus and Riz waiting in the lobby for them.

"Dave," grinned Riz, waving to him. "Dave, hi."

"Riz!" smiled Dave, weakly, shaking his hand. "Good to see you."

"Rufus – great job," said Dave.

Riz gestured to the reception desk. "Let's get you checked in. We've booked out the top floor of the hotel for the party, but there's been a bit of a mix-up and it seems Catie and Amy are now sharing."

Dave shrugged. "I'm sure they'll both survive."

"I'm going to let reception tell them," whispered Riz. "Now you'd better get some sleep Dave, we've blocked out late afternoon to rehearse for the Leaders' Debate tonight but before that you've got a morning full of visits and interviews."

"Sleep, yes. I intend to do that until the end of time."

"Sure, sure," said Riz. "We'll arrange your alarm call for six am."

"I'm sorry," said Dave. "I think I may have misheard you there. I thought you said six am."

"That's right," said Riz. "You're up for the BBC radio current affairs programme at seven am."

Dave checked his watch. "It's quarter past four. That's – that's not even two hours' sleep. That's ridiculous. Who's listening to current affairs at seven in the morning? Who presents the show, the milkman?"

"It's one of the most established political shows in the world –"

"I bet it is. Who's going to try to compete with it at that time in the morning – an intimate, sofa-based political chat show presented by a gang of badgers?"

"A cete," nodded Rufus.

Dave stared at him. "What?"

"The collective noun for badgers is a cete," said Rufus.

"Well, look," said Riz. "If you're too wiped out that's okay, we could put Rufus on again."

"No, it's fine," sighed Dave. "I need to get used to this. It's what politicians do. Excelsior Thorne probably only sleeps for twenty minutes a night, hanging upside down from a rafter somewhere. I'll just, you know, try to save some time by sleeping in the shower or something."

"WE RESCUED OTTO LAST YEAR. He has a head injury, which means he can only turn right."

The press-pack laughed, not at Otto tottering around in circles before flopping into a muddy pool, but at the irony. Alicia and Bart grimaced.

Excelsior Thorne was an hour into his visit to Acorn Otter Sanctuary. It had begun innocently enough, with a speech on family values at which a group of visiting school-children had been gratifyingly polite. Their teacher –

precisely the sort of chubby, late twenty-something female liberal that Thorne despised – had glared at him throughout. Fortunately, the clutch of journalists and photographers didn't seem to notice.

It was as he joined the children on a muddy, wellington-booted tour of the animal pens that things began fraying at the edges. It did not help that the weather turned, a wave of drizzle sweeping in and forcing everybody into their waterproofs. Then they met the otters.

Guybrush came first. He was a rescued otter, and a different species to those with whom he was penned. Thorne nodded, pointed at Guybrush's scars and asked if this inter-species housing created tensions. No, said the guide. Guybrush arrived with the scars, and in fact the otters welcomed him and helped him to heal. They now operated as one lodge.

After Guybrush, they met Wally and Bruno, who were Latvian and being conditioned for release in the UK. Otters were vital for British ecology, the guide pointedly explained, and 'migrant' otters had to be brought in from abroad. Then, as the children cooed over four handsome, silky Eurasian otters, Thorne tried to ask about foreign creatures damaging British wildlife.

Before the guide could answer, a small boy in a blue coat had looked up at him and sniffed, dispassionately: "*That's* the sort of thing that *people* cause."

"Well," began Thorne. "I think –"

"And there are simply *lots* of examples where introducing animals from other countries have helped us, mostly to fix *our* mistakes."

As metaphors flocked out of the animal pens to swirl around Thorne's head, each one captured for posterity by the press-pack, Thorne's face seemed relieved as they happened across an elderly otter in a pen on her own. A chance to talk about BEEF's key demographic, perhaps?

"And this is Mrs Bennett, our oldest resident," said the guide. "She's blind now, I'm afraid, and not very mobile."

Mrs Bennett wobbled over to the source of the noise, but tripped and fell to the delight of the schoolchildren. But as Thorne tried to weave his talking points into the conversation, the children began shrieking and pointing at a previous pen. Alicia looked up, to see Wally, Bruno and four other otters now involved in an activity that could be most delicately described as 'corporate'.

"What's Wally doing with Bruno?" asked the boy in the blue coat. "Why is he licking Bruno like that?"

"Well, they help each other to stay clean," said the guide. "It looks like Wally is helping Bruno to stay clean."

"I don't think I'd like anybody to clean me there," said the boy. "It is okay, then? For a boy to lick another boy like that?"

"Mr Thorne," said the children's teacher. "What would your response be to that question?"

"Oh no," murmured Bart.

"Well, I, er –" Thorne stumbled. "Look, we're for family values – you know, what people – I mean, er, otters – do in the privacy of their own dams. Homes –"

"So, it's okay?" said the boy, addressing Thorne directly. "Could they get married, then, Bruno and Wally?"

Thorne tried to smile, though merely the presence of plenty of teeth through curled lips did not – as Thorne's face demonstrated – constitute a smile. "Well, Wally and Bruno are animals, aren't they, er, boy? Animals can't get married."

The press-pack crowded around closely, as the nuances of BEEF's social agenda played out between its leader, a schoolboy and a platoon of cavorting otters.

"But what if they love each other? Could they get married if they were people? Could Wally and Bruno get married?"

Thorne paused as a camera flash lit up his face. "What's your name, young man?"

"I'm Caden."

"*Caden*? Really?"

"Yes! C-A-D-E-N!"

"For goodness sake, fine – Caden. How old are you?"

"I am five and three-quarters."

Thorne cleared his throat. "Well, Caden, in this country yes, right now, it's completely legal for two men to get married."

"Would you repeal that law, Mr Thorne?" Asked the teacher.

"Yes, yes we would. That's a manifesto promise."

Caden's lip started to quiver. "They can't get married?"

"Who, dear?" asked the guide.

"The man – the man says he'll stop Wally and Bruno getting married, even if they love each other!"

A fresh battery of camera flashes erupted as the boy burst into tears.

"We have to stop this," growled Bart. "Otto the spastic otter, bloody refugee weasels and these bummers – this has to end now!"

"They weren't bumming," said Alicia, evenly. "They were fellating."

"I don't care. Let's get him out of here, now, or he'll be off his game for TV tonight."

"That pap has just photographed Excelsior next to sign that reads 'warning – may bite'," said Alicia.

"Damn it!" snapped Bart. "This has been a disaster!"

Alicia smiled back at him. "Well, you know what they say, Bart. Never work with animals or children."

"What?" he snarled. "This was your idea!"

Alicia's eyes widened with mock incredulity. "Oh no, Bart. It was your idea, wasn't it? And I'm sure that Excelsior will ensure you get *all* the credit."

She walked smartly away, leaving Bart's shoulders heaving with fury.

DAVE STOOD at the window of Amy and Catie's room, his sleeves rolled up and tie loose, trying to look statesmanly.

"It isn't working," said Amy, munching on a slice of pizza.

"What isn't?" replied Dave, turning back to her.

Amy sat on her bed, surrounded by papers and pizza boxes. They had been rehearsing for the Leaders' Debate for some time. Dave felt he was doing quite well at defending HHHP policy – but they both agreed that he was struggling to land blows on opponents.

"Looking statesmanly," she said, taking a sip from a bottle of beer on the nightstand.

"How did you know I was trying to look statesmanly?"

Amy swallowed the beer. "You do a sort of, Jim-Hacker-distant-stare thing. I don't think anyone's used that expression since the Eighties."

Dave flopped into an easy chair and took a swig of beer from his own bottle. "I was going for Obama."

Amy let her eyes drop down him. "You don't quite have the, uh, physical presence for Obama, Dave."

Dave blinked. "Is this part of the test? I don't think

anyone's going to say that on the debate. 'Dave Williams, are you really tall enough to lead this country?'"

Amy smiled. "You're just a little more diminutive than Obama, that's all. But there are plenty of leaders who aren't that tall. You know, Putin, for one."

"Putin," echoed Dave. "Brilliant. Should I ride bare-chested to the debate?"

"I couldn't possibly comment, but I'm sure we can have your chest assessed for electability. Okay," Amy put down her beer and picked up a sheaf of papers. "So, Comrade, you're good on policy. But you're still not engaging well. You need to pick a fight up there. You'll get no broadcast time unless you can punch your way into the debate. And you're not winning votes if you're not speaking."

"I'm not really a fight-picky person – I like consensus, harmony."

"Well the consensus tonight is going to be that you've lost, unless you get a bit more pugilistic."

Dave frowned. "Maybe I *should* just take off my shirt."

"Now, look," said Amy. "Maybe all those other politician boys do what they want. But while you're under my care, you're not to go showing off those vote-winning nipples. Do you understand?"

Dave leaned forward. "Maybe it's that it doesn't feel real. Maybe when you're pretending to be the PM or the Leader of the Opposition you could, you know, do their voice or something?"

Amy raised an eyebrow. "You want me to do – *impressions*?"

"Just, you know, make it a bit more real."

Amy cleared her throat. "Okay, well, try this. Education is the most important issue in this election," she said, her voice notably deeper. "And we'll restore British education to the days when it taught our kids what they needed to know, so we could compete in the world, not the fads that they are currently indoctrinated with!"

Dave paused. "Is that the Prime Minister?"

"No," she whispered. "That was Excelsior Thorne. Come on!"

"Oh, right. Um – yes, well, Mr Thorne, you – that is, your policy, is – well."

Dave looked up, and his eyes met with Amy's. For a moment, just a moment, he thought he detected something else in there – something beyond the patient tutor, the political advisor. Something that wanted him to succeed. Something invested in him. Someone who truly saw him.

Dave stood up and coughed. "Mr Thorne, your education policy is about more than the curriculum. It's about marginalising foreign students for ideological reasons. Is *that* what you want to teach the children of Britain? That the answer to any difficult situation is *blame*?"

Amy's face broke into a broad smile. "Excellent!" she said. "There he is! And no partial nudity required!"

Dave took a slug of beer. "Thank you."

Amy looked at him for a moment, the smile remaining. "When you hit that channel, Dave – that groove, your whole being comes to life. That's when you become a leader. That's when you become statesmanly. Keep in that groove tonight, and the whole country's going to fall for you."

Dave's head dropped to one side. "Fall for me?"

"Vote for you. Is what I meant," said Amy suddenly, sitting up and dusting crumbs off herself. "You know, fall for you, in an electoral sense. They'll love you. Okay, we're nearly out of time – you need to get ready."

THE BOEING 777 rolled across the tarmac towards the terminal building, the orange lights of service vehicles flickering in the rain that streamed off the fuselage. With a loud whirr, an extendable gangway slithered towards the aircraft.

A stewardess opened the forward door with a *kah-chunk*, and the cabin filled with the scent of rain, jet fuel and fresh air. She smiled at the stand manager waiting on the other side of the door in his fluorescent yellow coat, and then stood with her colleagues to bid farewell to the passengers. The first, a tall, broad-shouldered man of colour who had slept most of the way in first class seat 3A, had to duck to move through the aircraft.

"Thank you, sir, have a good stay in England," she said.

"I will," said the Panther, stepping off the plane.

THE TELEVISION in Catie and Amy's room played mostly to itself while Catie sat at the desk, tapping furiously at a keyboard. Amy, meanwhile, peered into the mirror as she prepared herself for the evening.

"I like them," an elderly lady was telling an unseen news reporter from beneath a plastic rain bonnet. "I think they tell the truth."

The camera cut to a young man in a suit. "Yeah, well, they haven't got much experience – but does anyone when they first get into government, right?"

A burly-looking man in a dusty, plaid shirt and construction helmet was, predictably, the next in the *vox pops* segment. "Don't know really," he said. "Open to hearing a bit more about them. What's their name again? Happening, hope, hopping party? Something like that?"

Amy hung the second of her gold earrings and straightened her hair. She took a moment to look herself up and down. She had chosen a black, high-neck, cap-sleeved A-line dress. Smart, but elegant. She nodded, and glanced at her watch.

"Oh," she said. "I'd better check that the transport is all sorted out with the concierge."

"Knock yourself out," mumbled Catie.

"And just to confirm – Riz and I are going with Dave to the TV studios, everybody else is watching from here?"

"Yep," said Catie, without looking up.

Amy turned to leave, and then caught herself in the mirror one last time. "Does this make me look fat?"

Catie glanced at her and smiled. "No, of course not."

Amy smiled back, and opened the door. She stopped for a moment.

"Look, Catie – I know you don't like me," she said. "And it's all right. I get it."

Catie paused for a moment. "Okay," she said, sitting back in her chair. "Well, look at it from my perspective. It's not that I don't *like* you, Amy, I'm sure you're very nice – it's more that I don't *know* you. You've yet to win my trust. I mean, you show up, out of nowhere, and suddenly you're spending our money and making decisions within what, twenty minutes? It makes me uncomfortable."

"I understand."

"Dave trusts you. Clearly. And we want to support Dave, so I'll work with whatever his call is. But if it were up to me –"

Catie trailed off. Amy nodded.

"I do understand," she replied. "And I wanted to break the tension, by having this conversation. I just want you to know that I don't assume that I have your trust straight away. I'll earn it. I want you to know that."

Catie didn't reply, but nodded in acknowledgement.

"I should get downstairs," said Amy.

Catie sat forward again, her hands returning to her keyboard. "Dave's a really good person, Amy," she said. "And a very trusting one. He doesn't deserve to be let down."

Amy nodded again. "Well, thanks for your honesty, Catie, I appreciate it," she concluded, perhaps a little too quickly, and turned towards the corridor.

AMY THANKED the concierge and clip-clopped smartly across the lobby back to the elevators. She didn't see a man sitting in a small clutch of chairs spot her and leap up.

"Amy!" he called out. "Amy, hi!"

Amy turned to see Curtis Waugh, from one of the broadsheet dailies, stalking towards her.

"Curtis, hi," she said.

"It's great to see you," he beamed, towering over her in the fog of coffee-breath and ego that she had come to associate with a certain kind of journalist.

"You too," she said, as politely as she could.

"We've missed you since you've been hanging out with the hippies in Godforsakentown, Nowhereshire," he grinned. "What a career move! What happened?"

Amy maintained her smile. "Nothing *happened*, Curtis – it was the right time and the right move."

"I don't think anyone knew you were even looking for a new gig," he replied, with a glance around the lobby. "I suppose Downing Street should be worried, right? Not a good sign – fleeing the sinking ship, is it?"

"That's not for me to say."

"Still, though," his eyes settled on her, his grin dissolving into a smirk. "Why the *hippies*? Is that not, you know, self-relegation?"

"Maybe it is," she shrugged. "And maybe it isn't. Not that I'd expect you to understand, Curtis, but it's time for a totally new kind of political party. One you can believe in. Have you read the manifesto? These guys are the real thing. They're authentic, honest and the policies could really work. I mean, *really*. I haven't seen something like this for decades. Have you?"

Curtis half-laughed. "A few times – but never backed up with the kind of cash the hippies have got. Is that how they got you?"

Amy shook her head. "I've got a surprise for you – it's not about the money. It's about much more than that. Challenging concept, I know, for a journalist. Look, I've got to go – nice to see you. Watch David Williams on the Leaders' Debate tonight, Curtis. He'll bring the house down."

As she walked away, she took a deep breath. That was very convincing, she thought. Very convincing indeed.

Like she really believed it.

IT WAS early evening by the time that Martha arrived at the London cemetery, and the sun was starting to edge behind the tower blocks. She wasted no time parking her Mini – once the cheapest car she could find and now, apparently, a 'classic' – and hurried through the heavy iron gates.

Finding the cemetery in which Winstanley Mortimer was interred was easy, as a matter of public record. Finding the right grave, however, took a while, and she spent half an hour walking up and down the pathways between the headstones and monuments.

In a way, though, Martha enjoyed the stroll; there was a strange sort of peace to cemeteries. A calming sense of eternity, of gentle inevitability. Sadness, yes, but an oddly natural sadness. She passed a groundskeeper on the way, clad in dungarees and packing away a grass strimmer into a trolley. Maybe that would be a good job. Dignified, and bringing dignity to others. Cemeteries weren't such bad places to be.

She found Mortimer near a birch tree, its white limbs reaching up over the graves like ghostly arms. The headstone was cleaner, and the ground fresher, than its neighbours.

"Winstanley Mortimer," she read, calculating his age from the headstone at eighty-five. And that was it. Just a name and dates. A boilerplate headstone.

There was a bench under the tree, and she sat down to reflect.

It was very unusual, these days, to find such a wealthy individual in Britain with no online footprint at all. It still happened, of course, and Mortimer's age was consistent with one of the least represented groups – but it was not the norm. Meanwhile, Mortimer's companies and funds were offshore, mostly in places where public records were difficult or impossible to obtain.

Martha stood up again, turning these facts over in her mind, and walked back to the grave.

"Who are you?" she whispered.

She turned around, as crunching footsteps came towards her, to find the groundskeeper appearing with his trolley.

"Miss," he said. "Time to close up the cemetery, I'm afraid. You'll have to come back tomorrow."

"Oh," said Martha. "Sure. No problem. Listen – this grave, here, does it get many visitors?"

The groundskeeper took a step over and peered at the headstone. "Oh, Mr Mortimer – well, no, just you and the Prime Minister a few weeks ago."

Had Martha still been on the bench, she'd have fallen off it. As it was, her mind felt like it was falling off a bench, but her body refused to participate.

"*What*? I mean, pardon? The Prime Minister?"

The groundskeeper shrugged. "Yeah, well, I think it was him. It looked like him, and there was a load of people in suits. You know, secret-squirrel types. The car had those blue lights on. But that's the thing about a place like this. You find out who touches whose lives."

It suddenly seemed to get colder, and Martha pulled her coat around her. Instinctively, she glanced around.

"When was this?" She asked.

"Well, now, let's see – it was the day that Mr Mortimer first went in, so that was, what, a month ago?"

"Did you – did you hear anything that he said? How they knew each other?"

"Oh, now, miss – that would be confidential even if I did. That would be very wrong of me, to repeat anything."

Martha produced her ID card. "It's okay," she said. "I don't need to know your name or anything. I'm just working on a story. Important public interest. Maybe you can help?"

The groundskeeper shook his head. "I didn't hear anything, and please, this is not the place. Now, come on love, it's time to close up."

Dave stood at the mirror of his hotel room. He fastened his

cufflinks and stared at the man in the dark, pristine suit and smart, salmon-pink tie looking back at him. For a moment, he wondered who it was. Had he changed that much these last few weeks that it was hard to recognise himself? Or was he just tired? The latter was certainly true – earlier he had looked down at the dozens of sheets of talking points on the floor, and thought about what an inviting place it looked like to sleep.

There was a knock at the door, and Dave opened it to reveal Amy.

"Hello, No-bama," she smiled.

"Ah, great," replied Dave, stepping aside to let her in. "My pre-debate confidence-boost has arrived."

"Just getting you fired up to take on your sparring partners tonight. And, dropping by to let you know the car is waiting outside."

"Sure. Well, I'm ready. Any last words of wisdom?"

Amy took hold of his tie and straightened it. "Remember," she said. "Voice as deep as possible, sit up so you look tall, speak as simply as possible. All these things are associated with higher approval ratings."

"Got it," nodded Dave.

"You can do this, Dave," she said, lightly tapping his chest with her finger. "Think positively, engage, and those dreams of Buckingham Palace and the Queen might, one day, be more than dreams."

Dave's eyes widened. "How did you –"

"Dillon told me," she smiled.

"How much did he, er, tell you, Amy?"

They paused, their eyes meeting. It was a pause that went on for a good few beats longer than the platonic deadline.

"You look good," said Amy.

"So do you," said Dave.

There was another pause.

"No, ah, need for the – shirtlessness," said Amy, her voice trailing away.

For years after, Dave would wish he could remember the seconds that followed. But he seemed barely aware of them as they happened, never mind adequately recording them for posterity. Suddenly, and in a haze that left his head swooping, his lips and Amy's were together.

And then as quickly as it had happened, it was over, and they were taking a step back from each other. Amy blushed, and straightened her hair. Dave suddenly became very aware of his hands and the lack of anywhere appropriate to put them.

"Well," he said, realising he was looking at his feet as much as her face.

"Well," she said. She cleared her throat. "You'd better get down to the lobby – I'll follow on, I've just got some, well. Things to do."

"Yes," nodded Dave, somewhat too enthusiastically. "Yes, of course. Yes. I'll see you in the car. Yes."

A FEW MILES AWAY, the black BEEF Mercedes swept over the Thames and into the neon-lit Hammersmith night.

Alicia Rhodes' finger hovered, mid-sentence, over her iPad. She had to admit, she was caught off-guard.

"What's the matter, Alicia?" said Bart. "Did someone hit your pause button?"

Alicia rested the iPad on her lap. "No, I just wasn't expecting that to be your advice. Of *course* we should distance ourselves."

Bart shook his head. "I don't care if Satan and his grand demonic army say they're voting for BEEF, we don't distance ourselves from supporters."

"Who is this guy, anyway?" growled Thorne.

"He's a European fascist leader who condones violence against migrants and religious minorities, and is giving you his full support on social media," replied Alicia, but directing her answer toward Bart. "He's been arrested twice and is currently under investigation by the French police. His stamp of approval on us is going to be seen as our stamp of approval on him, if you don't issue a statement."

Bart shrugged. "Tomorrow's chip-papers."

"Excelsior?"

Thorne's generous lips curled downwards. "People are frustrated," he said.

Alicia looked out of the window. "I don't think violence, and condoning violence, is the answer."

"Well, boys will be boys," said Bart.

The car fell silent, leaving only the radio news in the air.

"And in Sandport, we understand that the latest polls show David Williams, the leader of the HHHP, with a comfortable lead," said the presenter.

"Turn that off. I don't need this heckling," snapped Thorne. "I need to focus."

Bart leaned forward and switched off the radio. "Just knock this out of the park," he said. "Then we'll zoom back in on Sandport. We can put everything we've got into it."

Thorne nodded.

"Jack yourself up to eleven," went on Bart. "The Full Thorne. Remember, you're selling the cure to fear. So, make sure everybody watching knows they have that illness. Smash this, and you'll smash the HHHP. You'll smash Williams."

Thorne looked out of the window and grunted with approval. "He's going down, tonight."

POLICE SIRENS ANNOUNCED the prime ministerial car like a fanfare, and it swerved into the grounds of the television centre in a firework display of blue and red emergency lights.

"Well, Duncan," smiled the Prime Minister, as the car came to a stop and suited Special Branch officers approached it. "Let's see how Mr David Williams has shaped up under Amy's tutelage. I'm rather looking forward to this."

The door opened and the PM stepped out, as Starling nodded to himself.

"Indeed," he said.

AS THE PARTY leaders converged at the BBC, Dave still sat with Riz in the car outside the hotel.

"Where is she?" he said.

Riz glanced at his watch again. "She's not answering her phone. Look, she'll have to catch us up, Dave," he said. "We've got to go. Let's drive on please," he added, to the driver.

"Right-o."

The car moved off, and Dave watched the hotel slip away.

"Sure," he said, turning back to face forward. "Okay. Focus. Okay."

The BBC car slipped out into the traffic, and headed for the Leaders' Debate.

TRUMPET FLOURISHES and orchestral stabs overlaid metallic, computer-generated political rosettes that flew low over a satellite map of Britain and plunged down towards south London.

"Seven days until the General Election," boomed a gravelly voice. "Seven main political parties. Seven party leaders. And only one vote that counts – yours. Welcome to the General Election Leaders' Debate."

The screen dissolved into an azure-blue stage, and the camera swooped over seven figures standing behind thin, modern lecterns glowing with their party colours and completing a rainbow semi-circle on the stage.

"Guys," said Catie. "It's starting."

They were in Rufus' room, surrounded by beers and kebab wrappers. Party staffers stood by the walls, tapping into their glowing phone screens. Catie sat in one of the few chairs, Rufus and Dillon cross-legged on the bed.

The audience applauded on cue, and the final strains of the opening music came in to land.

"Good evening," said the female host, a well-known newscaster. "Welcome to the Leaders' Debate. Tonight, the seven leaders of the highest-polling parties will attempt to convince you why your votes should go to their candidates. After a brief opening statement by each leader, the candidates will respond to a series of specially-chosen audience questions. After that, the second half of the programme will be a free debate, where we can hear the leaders compare and contrast their views."

"And we're off," said Dillon, folding his arms.

"Excelsior Thorne," said the host. "You won the coin toss, so you begin with your opening statement."

Thorne looked at the camera, and his face filled the screen.

"Ew," said Rufus. "If there was ever an indictment of high-definition, it's that."

"Friends," said Thorne. "You face a huge choice in this election. And that's an important thing, choice. That's why we fought two world wars. To have *choice*. And you know, something that none of these other parties will admit is that they don't want to give you choice. They want to make decisions for you. The establishment has told you what to value, and how to live, and has made you accept the priorities that they want. Well, we're different. We say that you, the British people, are the priority – over all others."

HER HOTEL ROOM door clicked open, and Amy rushed in, failing to hold back fat, unwelcome tears. She snatched some tissues, with which she inadvertently smeared her mascara across her face like war-paint, and threw her suitcase on the bed.

It only took a moment to stuff her things into the case, write a note on the hotel stationery, and slip off her evening shoes. She replaced them with sneakers, slipped the note into an envelope and wiped her eyes again.

She seized her bag, left the room and after slipping the note under Dave's door, was out of the hotel and into the night.

Amy Cordell was gone in minutes.

THE PARTY LEADERS had argued about the economic deficit,

immigration, the National Health Service and European policy. The Prime Minister and the Leader of the Opposition had skirmished about defence. Excelsior Thorne had been set upon by most of the other leaders on education, and even by the Welsh nationalist leader after an unwise remark about Bangor.

And through it all, Dave had said almost nothing, politely nodding or grimacing as appropriate.

"Come on Dave!" shouted Catie at the television. "Get involved!"

"You know," the Prime Minister was saying, "a lot of the people on this stage have laudable aspirations. But very few have the experience for the complex and hugely important job of *government*. We've heard unworkable policies, and questionable grips on policy – especially on economics and foreign matters. We are only part-way through our plan for Britain, and risking it on some of the ideas we've heard tonight is something I implore you not to do."

"Come on Dave," whispered Catie.

Dave opened his mouth and started to speak, but the Leader of the Opposition was quicker and, more importantly, louder and bolder.

"Ladies and gentlemen, I think it's very brave of the Prime Minister to promise 'more of the same.' More of what, exactly? More bungled wars? More chaos in the civil service? More policy u-turns? I think there's quite a bit there that we could do with *less* of!"

Catie was on her feet now. "Come on, Dave! Speak! Speak, Dave!"

"The experience that matters is in defending the rights of the British people," said Thorne's oily voice, as the camera cut to him. "I don't think that we need experience at fudging immigration, compromising on trade deals, eroding family values in favour of whatever the liberal flavour of the month is."

And then, Catie heard someone she recognised.

"Mr Thorne has a point – but as usual, it is warped," said Dave, the camera settling on him. "The substance is that experience may be important, but trust and honesty are most important. And yet, that's where he – and the other parties – are going wrong."

"Hurrah!" shouted Rufus. "Go Dave!"

Thorne chuckled. "And where is the expertise in your party, David? Your most important job was a brief stint putting baubles on Christmas trees in a factory, wasn't it?"

The camera, with a perfect cutaway, caught Dave's eyes wide and fearful, his mouth frozen.

"Oh no – I can't watch," said Rufus.

WHEN HE HAD STEPPED onto the stage, Dave had no idea how hot the studio lighting would be. Underneath his jacket, he was a swamp of perspiration. And the lights were bright too – he could barely see the audience. The last time he had sweated this profusely had been a job interview, but at least then there hadn't been the bright lights of a near-death experience. Just a puzzled-looking baker wondering why he wasn't answering a basic question about hand-washing.

And now, the whole country was looking at him. The studio was silent. He could see at least four cameras pointing at his face. The other six men and women were staring his way. Thorne was sneering. Dave's hands felt clammy. His lips parted slightly, but nothing happened.

The second of silence stretched out longer, and longer. And then, something flickered across his memory. It was

Catie, sitting in Green House. And then Michael, sitting in the back of a chip shop in Seahaven. And Amy; Amy looking directly into his soul.

Dave let his eyes rove across the other party leaders, before settling back on Thorne. When he spoke, he almost didn't recognise his own voice.

"You know what I see around me, Mr Thorne?" he said. "I see a banker, a lawyer, career politicians and a frankly predatory businessman. And do you know what you've all got in common? It's that you have *no idea* what life is like for real people."

Thorne laughed. "A personal attack? That's how the HHHP contributes to the Leaders' Debate?"

Dave waved him away and turned to the camera. "No, wait, this is important. You see, all these men and women know how to tug the strings of ordinary people. They know how to make us think that they have the answers – but they're at best ideological, at worst fig-leaves for the interests that pull *their* strings. But this time, you can put a different kind of party into Downing Street. One that understands what real life is, understands you, and won't sell you to its masters. We won't pretend that we have all the answers, or try to manipulate you. And when you hear someone like Excelsior Thorne mocking jobs like the ones I held, it tells you more about him and his party than his manifesto ever will."

An enthusiastic wave of applause burst across the audience.

"I think we can share your frustration, David," said the Leader of the Opposition, cutting in over the applause. "But government needs a policy platform, not just positive intent. And while no right-thinking person should agree with Excelsior's stance on immigration –"

"Why not?" snapped Thorne.

The Leader of the Opposition tried to repeat himself, as Thorne barked his challenge again and again.

"Okay," said Dave. "Let's take immigration as an example, then – so you leaders, all of you, hear that half the country is worried about it. But you've also got access to the analysis that shows how critical it is to the economy, how beneficial it is, and the horrors of the alternative. And yet, you don't respect the electorate by engaging with them, thinking 'okay, so, how are we going to persuade them of its benefits?' You just borrow BEEF policies; because all that matters is the vote, right? No matter how dangerous the policies are. You're as bad as the bankers who sell mortgages that they know the customers can't afford. You're selling policies the country can't afford."

There was a slow, solitary clap from somewhere on the stage, and the camera panned back to Thorne, whose sarcastic applause was the first for any television general election debate in Britain.

"Well done," said Thorne. "Well done, Mr Williams – the liberal elite speaks. They don't want to carry out *your* wishes, Britain – they want *you* to rubber-stamp *theirs!*"

Dave smiled. "This phrase, 'liberal elite', is remarkable Mr Thorne, when I think about those on this stage. There's nothing elite about the Happening Happy Hippy Party, but *you*, sir, are the *literal* elite."

Elsewhere in London, a hotel room full of hippies cheered with everything in them, and the writers of tomorrow's headlines began to idly consider which hippy-related puns would be necessary to cover the HHHP's increasingly inevitable poll rise.

☮

"GAVIN MILTON IS live in Sandport now, outside the HHHP's campaign headquarters, to which we understand David Williams is returning this evening. Gavin, what's the party response to opinion polls implying that David Williams won tonight's debate?"

"Well, James, the HHHP's campaign seems an almost unstoppable machine now. Sources in the City even told us that although some industries remain sceptical and even opposed to them, others are privately calling the HHHP's suite of economic policies more viable, and more laden with opportunity, than the government's. They have even acquired a name – 'Dave-onomics'. So, it may be no surprise then that the polls tonight are showing the party have been catapulted to as much as twenty-five per cent, putting it within a hair's breadth of both the government and the Opposition. We understand, in fact, that the hashtag 'I'm with Dave' is now trending on social media."

The Prime Minister switched the television off, and smiled at Starling.

"Well, Duncan," he said. "I do believe that Amy has been most successful. Excellent work. You'll pass on my compliments, I hope?"

"Of course," said Starling. "When I next speak to her. She's not picking up my calls at the moment."

The Prime Minister sat down at his desk. "Well, no matter."

"What now?"

"Time to spring the trap," replied the Prime Minister, opening a drawer and removing a new, boxed mobile phone. He opened the cellophane wrapper, and slid out the cardboard tray containing the handset.

"What's that?" asked Starling, as the Prime Minister

loaded the battery into the phone and stripped off the protective film.

"Reassuringly disposable," he replied, keying in a number from a piece of paper on the desk. "Hello, is that the National Crime Agency? Yes, I would like to report a very serious financial crime, please. No, you don't need my name."

7

The Volkswagen campervan swerved into the single parking space outside HHHP Central, and Dave leapt out before it even finished coming to a halt.

It had been some weeks since he'd been here, but he noticed neither the growth of ivy across the wall, nor that the potted plants outside – so lovingly tended by Catie – were now withered and unkempt. He further failed to register, as he checked his phone for the seventeenth time in an hour, that the door was already open.

"Hey," he said, upon entering. "What are you doing here?"

Dillon sat on the floor, surrounded by cardboard boxes, into one of which he had just finished placing the HHHP official teapot with great care.

"HHHP Central needs to be locked up," said Dillon, rising to his feet and brushing his hair out of his face. "Riz says that apparently it's turned into some sort of shrine. Tourists keep nicking bits of it as souvenirs. They've even taken that old microwave that was rusting by the door. I think they thought it was art."

Dave glanced around. HHHP Central felt both alien and familiar. "Is Amy here? Has she been here?"

Dillon shook his head. "No, what's going on? Are you okay? You look terrible."

"Hello?" called a voice from outside, and Rufus and Catie appeared in the doorway.

"Dave, there you are! Why aren't you in London?" asked Catie. "I'm getting a lot of calls – you've missed all your appointments and now you're *here*? Riz is fighting fires all over the place!"

"What's going on?" said Rufus.

"Amy's gone," said Dave. "There was a note. I found it this morning. It just said, 'I'm sorry'. That's it. She won't answer her calls, nothing. She's vanished."

"Oh dear," said Catie. "I'm sorry to hear that."

"No you're not," replied Dave. "You're pleased. I can hear it in your voice."

Catie shook her head. "Not at all. I just – I'm just not surprised, Dave. I'm sorry."

"Maybe she just needed some time to herself?" suggested Rufus. "Sometimes I get jolly cross and I need to go for one of my special alone-time naked jogs."

Dillon's eyes widened. "Rufus, I –"

"In the middle of an election campaign?" said Dave, his failure to engage Rufus testimony to the heat of his concern. "She's a pro! She wouldn't do that!"

"Maybe it's only for an hour or two?" went on Rufus. "You know, she's just gone to sit under the stairs or something?"

"She's not a cat, Rufus," said Dave.

"Dave, we can't let this dominate the campaign," said Catie, putting her hand on his arm. "Shall I make you some tea? We need to get you back out on the trail. We're so close."

Dillon was regarding Dave through narrow eyes. "Something happened, didn't it? Something – extracurricular?"

Dave swallowed. "No. I mean yes. No. Yes."

"You went special naked jogging together!" Rufus beamed.

Catie dropped her hand. "Dave!"

Dillon laughed, and then the front door flew off its hinges and crashed to the floor in a puff of splinters.

"Police!" shouted a lot of very loud, very angry people, as men in helmets and Kevlar poured into the room. "Stay where you are!"

Dave thought he heard Catie scream, but then he realised it was Rufus as two officers pushed him to the floor, and chained his wrists together with decisive clicks of steel.

"What the hell is going on?" said Dillon's voice, muffled as his face collided with the wall.

Dave opened his mouth to protest, but the words did not come as quickly to his mouth as the floor did, and he found himself pinned down beneath a mountainous human clad in paramilitary black.

As quickly as the chaos had arrived it subsided, and there was silence apart from the electronic slurps of the officers' radios. Blue lights flickered through the open doorway, and two bald, broad-shouldered gentlemen in suits and raincoats stepped over the battered door and into the room.

"I want the whole building searched," said the older of the two from beneath a moustache that seemed to quiver like a nervous hamster as he spoke. "Though I doubt that'll take long. Which one of you is David Williams?"

"Me," mumbled Dave from the floor.

The younger of the two – an assessment that Dave

derived from a slightly more lustrous moustache – flashed a warrant card at him.

"Good morning Mr Williams," he said. "I'm Detective Sergeant Pike and I'm arresting you on suspicion of money laundering."

"Money laundering?" said Rufus. "That's preposterous! And I should know, I'm the treasurer!"

The older detective leaned in to Rufus, inspecting his face. The hamster moustache twitched with rising energy. "And you are?"

"I am The Honourable Rufus Lane-Seymour, and I demand to see your superior officer!"

At this, the hamster erupted into such spasms that it looked like it was trying to free itself from the detective's face. "Ah yes, Lane-Seymour! You're nicked too."

"Boss," said one of the uniformed officers from the kitchenette. "Found something."

"What is it, constable?"

The officer was poking experimentally at several shrink-wrapped blocks, dark in colour. "Some kind of organic, herbal matter."

"That's tea!" said Dillon. "Those are tea leaves!"

"Yours, are they?" said Pike. It was more a statement than a question.

"Well, yes –"

Pike gestured to the van. "Bring him in too. Possession with intent to supply."

"Possession with intent to supply?" Bellowed Dillon. "Supply what? Tea? What do you think I am, a branch of frigging Whittards?"

With loud protests and threats of legal action, Dave, Rufus and Dillon were dragged out of the building into the sun, and thrown into police vans with much clanging of doors.

Catie stood alone in the corner, recording the police search on her phone, the room silent apart from the grunting of the officers as they dismantled HHHP Central.

DAVE TOOK A DEEP BREATH. "I've told you," he said. "We were left the money in Winstanley Mortimer's will. I'd never seen nor heard of it before."

He sat in a tiny interview room, his sleeves rolled up to his elbows. A cassette player whirred quietly by his side. The hot, stagnant air of the breeze-blocked chamber carried the odour of vomit, stale sweat and cleaning fluid.

DS Pike sat across the table. Another officer, whose name was Edwards, had replaced the hamster moustache and was making notes on a pad. Harry Fisk was next to Dave, and had a pad too, but had so far used it solely to draw intricate doodles of handcuffs.

"Okay," said Pike. "So, can you explain, then, why before it was wired to Mr Mortimer's account, the money made its way through a network that included a People's Bank of Kundunga account in your name, Mr Williams?"

"No," insisted Dave. "I don't know. I've never had a bank account in another country. I've barely got one in this one. They keep sending me angry letters."

Edwards sniffed. "A history of financial irregularity, eh?"

"No, it's been *very* regular. I have had almost no money in almost every year."

Okay, Mr Williams," said Pike. "Look. You're in a lot of trouble, here. You could be charged with money laundering, and of ten *million* pounds, Mr Williams. There's a heavy sentence attached to that. And that's if you're even prosecuted here – how would you like to stand trial in Africa? I'll tell you now, Belmarsh would be like a children's ball-pit filled with marshmallows compared to what goes on in those African prisons. I expect they'd have a field day with a lovely boy like you."

"But I've never been to Africa!"

Pike opened a folder in front of him and selected a sheet from a leaf of papers.

"Here is a copy of a Malawian driving license in your name," he said, placing it front of Dave. "That's your face, isn't it?"

"Well, yes, but –"

"And one passport, also in your name, also with that familiar face," said DS Pike, producing another sheet. "These are the documents that were used to open the account. Is that you?"

"Okay, it looks like me, yes – but those aren't mine!"

Pike waited a beat, staring at Dave.

"Do you know what a 'predicate offence' is, Mr Williams?"

"Was that the thing in *Minority Report*?"

"No. It is the criminal offence from which the money that's been laundered derives. Would you like to tell us where this money came from?"

"I don't know!" said Dave. "Seriously, a month ago I'm just Dave Williams, sitting at home in front of the telly, and now I'm Keyser Soze?"

"What do you know about blood diamonds, Mr William? The diversion of foreign aid? The looting of fragile states? Drug trafficking?"

"I don't know anything about any of those things!"

"Have you ever heard the names Obi and Uba?"

"Uber? The taxi people?"

Pike smirked. "How about we look at it this way, Mr Williams? Ten million pounds from a portfolio of serious criminal activities in West Africa disappears into a warren of bank accounts, funds and companies and then resurfaces in the campaign fund of a political party. What does that sound like to you, Mr Williams?"

There was a silence, and Pike let it hang.

"I need a lawyer," said Dave.

"I'm right here," nodded Fisk.

Dave glanced at him. "I mean a real one."

IT WAS FRONT-PAGE NEWS. Not just in the UK, but in every European nation except Iceland, where the lead singer of Icelandick – Iceland's number one boy-band – was embroiled in a complex controversy involving an overdue parking ticket, the true authorship of their hit song 'plinky-binky-boo', and something about a seagull.

The newspapers that had once exalted the HHHP now reported the arrests of the party leadership on suspicion of money laundering and drug supply. Britain's most notorious right-wing tabloid even published a front-page piece on the HHHP for the first time, noting that one of Catie's grandparents was Hungarian and describing Rufus' month on a kibbutz some years ago as a visit to a 'Middle Eastern training camp'.

Catie and Rufus sat in HHHP Central later that afternoon, in silence. The room was a mess, with upended chairs, torn rosettes and broken mugs strewn across it. The police hadn't tidied up after themselves. They've even left the taps running.

Rufus had been released on bail not long after the police realised that he was not a real accountant. This had become clear early in his interview, when Rufus was asked to show them the books and he'd asked whether they wanted to see his Le Carre or Grisham first.

Upon returning to HHHP Central and Catie, he had placed a wooden table up against the doorway to keep out the press, the door itself lying sadly on the floor where the police had left it. He sat on the sofa now, cross-legged and chain-smoking. Catie's knees were drawn up to her chin, deep in thought.

The silence broke as the table against the doorway began to wobble, and then shunted into the room. Dillon, bruised and shivering in the evening cold, stood in the doorway.

Catie and Rufus looked up at him.

He swallowed. "It really was tea," he said.

Catie leapt up and wrapped her arms around him, burying her face into his chest.

Rufus sat back in the sofa and nodded. "What now?"

Dillon closed the door, and Catie helped him replaced the table against a tumult of flashing lights and shouts from press photographers. "I don't know," he said. "This is madness. Dave can barely launder clothes, never mind money."

"They raided Green House, too. Apparently Riz has closed it and sent everybody home. The police took all the servers and most of the computers."

"Well," said Dillon with half a smile. "It won't take a genius to analyse the accounts. Fifty quid a month for four years and then ten million three weeks ago."

Rufus stubbed out his cigarette and fished in his pockets for another. "My faith in the Fuzz is not high, given that

Starsky and Hutch earlier mistook five kilos of lapsang souchong for Class C drugs."

"Will they let Dave out on bail, like Rufus?" asked Catie.

Dillon took off his coat and headed for the kettle. "I don't know. Depends whether they consider him a flight-risk, I suppose, and whether they're going to charge him. Have we found Amy?"

"No," replied Catie. "She is, funnily enough, nowhere to be found just as our world caves in."

Rufus lit another cigarette. "Should we make some kind of statement? To the press? I don't think they're going anywhere. They've got flasks. I think they're planning to make a night of it."

"And say what?" said Dillon, filling up the kettle. "We don't know anything. We can't deny stuff if we don't know what we're denying."

"We can give a general one," said Catie. "I can take care of that. But we need a plan. Dillon, you're the Glorious Leader now. What do we do?"

Dillon looked around the room, the floor strewn with broken furniture and smashed crockery.

"Can we still fight the campaign?" he asked as his eyes roamed over the mess.

"They have asset freezing orders on us," said Rufus. "I don't think so. We can't get to our money."

"Well," replied Dillon. "We can still fight here in Sandport, we can focus in on Dave's campaign here. We don't need big bucks for that. We can't stay silent and give up – if we do that, it looks like it's true."

Dillon took a few steps forward, bending over to pick up his favourite blue mug. As he did so, the handle and a sizeable chunk remained on the floor. He inspected the china in his hands. "We've been set up," he murmured. "We need to find out by whom."

"Well, that's the only way to clear our names," said Rufus, exhaling. "And I'd say that Harry Fisk is a good starting point."

"I'd throw Amy Cordell in there too," added Catie. "Mind you, I'd just throw her. Hang on – Martha Lewandowski. She was asking questions about Winstanley Mortimer."

Dillon leaned back against the sink. "Yes – maybe she knows something. Maybe she can help."

Catie nodded. "Exactly. Rufus, you try to find Amy, Dillon you call Riz and plan our media counter-offensive. I'll go see Martha and then join you."

"Okay!" said Dillon. "I'll go outside to call, I'll get better reception – you take the campervan!"

They charged out into the afternoon, igniting a blast of camera flashes and shouts from excitable paparazzi, leaving Rufus standing in HHHP Central.

"Right," he said to himself, clapping his hands together. "Right! Find Amy! Find Amy. Find – Amy," he trailed off, looking around.

The room was silent.

"Find Amy," he murmured, looking experimentally behind the sofa and checking, for reasons clear only to him, the sink.

"WE MUST WORK TOGETHER, across the political spectrum, to stamp on the tendrils of corruption," said Excelsior Thorne to the assembled television cameras. "There can be no place for craven dishonesty in the representation of the people. I applaud the diligent efforts of our law enforcement community, and if these matters are true, trust in our fine judicial system to ensure that propriety is restored."

Alicia and Bart stood either side of him, nodding solemnly while a thin ripple of applause from a cluster of BEEF supporters concluded Thorne's words. It was a recorded statement – one that the networks could roll out at their leisure over the course of the news cycle. Alicia much preferred these, as the statement could simply be re-recorded in the event of an error. Live news was always more of a risk with politicians, where any tendency to wander from the script could result, at best, in the creation of completely new words and at worst, completely new policy.

One of the cameramen looked up. "Great, that's great Mr Thorne, thanks a lot."

"Thank you," said Thorne, and turned around to step into the Boatman's Arms.

The cheers and applause in here, however, were deafening. Thorne smiled broadly and waved as he made his way to the bar through a gleeful crowd. He raised his hands in an appeal for quiet.

"Friends, friends," he said, wrapping one hand around a pint that the smiling landlord had already poured for him. "What a momentous day! The hippies have been exposed for the frauds they are – there will be no more pulling the wool over the eyes of the electorate! Today, witness the beginning of the end for the wishy-washy, short-sighted liberal agenda!"

There were renewed cheers, and Thorne took a victorious swig of beer.

"Well," he said, turning to Bart and Alicia. "I'm actually impressed. I didn't think they had it in them. Did you?"

Alicia shook her head. "No, and I think that's what bothers me."

"Bothers you?"

Alicia smiled briefly at the landlord as she received a gin and tonic, and turned back to Thorne. "It's just – I mean, multi-million pound money laundering? The Happening Happy Hippy Party? They've been helped, I'm sure. There's something bigger here."

Bart didn't look up from his phone, upon which he was frenziedly tapping. "Globalist conspiracy, Alicia," he murmured. "They're the pawns of powerful puppet-masters, aiding and abetting the proliferation of the bankrupt liberal regime."

Alicia almost rolled her eyes. "Well, yes, Bart – that was the point I was making."

Bart slipped his phone into his pocket. "Enjoy your beer, Excelsior – because we need to ramp up for this final stretch. Maximum effort."

Thorne blinked over the rim of his glass. He swallowed. "What? Didn't you see the numbers? This constituency is just a two-horse race, and the other horse is in prison. What are they going to do with two days to go?"

"So, we make sure we win," said Bart. "Tomorrow's the Coastal FM 'Sandport Decides' event. There'll be thousands listening in. Without Williams, I don't know who the HHHP will send to give their speech – nobody any good, I bet. It'll be your afternoon. Bring your A-game, and leave the other candidates to me."

CATIE WALKED into the Duck and Fiddle and found Martha easily enough, sitting tucked away in a far corner with a glass of something clear and neat that didn't look quite like water. And she didn't look good, thought Catie as she walked towards her. Pale, even nervous.

"Hi," said Catie, pulling out a chair and sitting down. "Not heard from you in a few days, Martha."

Martha took a slurp of not-water. "Yeah, well," she said. "I've been busy."

"What are you drinking?"

"Vodka."

"Want another?"

Martha shook her head. "What do you want?"

"You've seen the news, right?"

"I knew there was something dodgy about that donation, Catie," she said, holding her glass with both hands.

"Well," sighed Catie. "It turns out you were right. But we had nothing to do with it. It just came, one day. Dave got a letter from his lawyer. And now he's in custody."

Martha glanced beyond Catie, to the door.

"Yes, well," she said, brushing auburn hair out of her face. "Are you going on record? Do you want to tell me something about it?"

Catie paused, and then reached out and gently touched Martha's hand. "Are you all right, Martha? You seem – distracted."

Their eyes met for the briefest of moments. "Yes, of course," replied Martha, pulling her hand away. "Well?"

Catie straightened up. "*Well*," she repeated. "I was actually going to ask you some questions. I know you've been looking into us, looking into this money. What do you know about where it came from? About Winstanley Mortimer – who he was, who he knew?"

Martha's eyes caught Catie's again with those last few words.

"Who?" She pressed. "Who did he know? What do you know about him, Martha?"

Martha took another gulp of vodka. "I need to protect my sources, Catie."

"You know you can trust me."

"Can I?" replied Martha. "Can I really?"

Catie sighed. "Don't start this again, Martha –"

Martha shrugged. "I just remember, that's all. People's past behaviour is the best predictor of their futures."

She was drunk, thought Catie. She was always combative when she was drunk. "That was, like, two years ago –"

"Nineteen months."

"– And this is totally different. This isn't some stupid mistake at a party. This is serious, you know we're not the kind of people who would get mixed up in this stuff. And you know that Excelsior Thorne is basically going to own this town on Thursday if you don't help us. So, help us. What do you know? And why are you on your – I don't know, maybe third – vodka?"

Martha was quiet for a while, letting her eyes settle on Catie's. Her expression betrayed a war between her suspicion and her curiosity; the two traits that had got her this far now wrestling each other for control while her heart shrieked and wept drunkenly from the side-lines about it 'not being worth it'.

Curiosity won.

"Okay," she said. "Here's the deal. I'll help you – but if you guys aren't guilty, if this *is* a set-up, I get the story. Front page, *Sandport Chronicle*. Nobody else."

Catie nodded. "I'll even help you get the best photos."

"And this means nothing between you and me, Catie, okay?" said Martha. "This is just business."

"Just business. Honestly, there's nothing between us. I'm not interested in you at all. That couldn't be further from my mind. I'm totally over you. You're not even on my radar."

Martha stared at her.

"Well, you know what I mean."

"Okay. Well," Martha took a breath. "Here's what I know. Winstanley Mortimer has no discernible connections with anyone. There are just companies and funds – lawyers, investment accounts, go-betweens. No family, no friends, no colleagues anywhere to be found. Except one."

"Who?"

Martha leaned in. "The Prime Minister."

"The *Prime Minister*?" Catie nearly shouted.

"Shh! Yes, the Prime Minister. He visited Mortimer's grave. I don't know why, or what the connection is – but I reckon the source is pretty reliable. The PM *was* there."

Catie reached over and took a gulp of Martha's vodka. "What does that mean?" she asked.

"I don't know," said Martha. "At least, not yet. But your FCU people have some pretty amazing tech. Even access to satellites and stuff. If we could use them, we might be able to find something."

"I'll make some calls," said Catie, slipping out her phone. "And if Amy isn't at the centre of this whole thing, I'll eat my bloody nose-stud," she added, under her breath.

THE PRIME MINISTER'S JAGUAR cruised through the London night, flanked by police motorcycles and sparkling blue emergency lights. In the back, he and Starling listened to a young Downing Street analyst on speakerphone.

"So, in the round, the HHHP are down from twenty-seven points to ten," said the analyst's voice. "We're up five, which gives us a good lead over the Opposition, who don't seem to have won back those who went HHHP. There's a very small, evenly-distributed increase across some of the other parties – but the big winner here is now 'don't know', up ten points, and 'won't vote', up eight. When we run the analysis, it looks like we'll land on a small majority for us, sir. But a majority, nonetheless."

"What does that mean for turnout?" asked Starling.

"We're on course for the lowest turnout – and the widest distribution of votes across opposition parties – in modern political history."

"Excellent, thank you," said the Prime Minister, turning off the phone. "There we are, Duncan! We've done it! We've disenchanted the swing voters, and split up the unflush-ables who insist on voting against us between the opposi-tion parties. See? Piece of cake."

It was good news, of course. Politics was better from the leather-bound seats of a Jaguar, pulled through the night by the smooth purr of a V8. Returning to opposition would mean the end of perks like that. But Starling couldn't ignore the sleepless nights and twists in his gut.

"What about the police?" He said. "I'm worried about the police investigation."

The Prime Minister waved his hand. "Oh, relax Duncan – that won't go anywhere. We'll have that quietly ended in a few weeks. Not in the public interest, that sort of thing. Hardly appropriate for the police to investigate political parties, is it? Where would all that end?"

"But what if they find something, sir?"

"They won't. And even if they do, all the evidence is off in mad places that are jolly difficult to access. Interpol, Mutual Legal Assistance – they'll all struggle to extract anything. It'll be like one of those machines where you try to grab toys with a big claw," The Prime Minister made a claw gesture with his hand to illustrate his point.

"I see," said Starling.

"No, the police have already obligingly served their purpose. The HHHP is dead, and the electorate are confused and demoralised. Cheer up, Duncan, old boy! Only two sleeps left and it's champagne and speeches! I think I'll have the plane upgraded this time. It's all a bit business class. I think we can do better than that."

"Look at the state of this place," said Dave, as he turned on a light and let his eyes take in the chaos of HHHP Central.

Fisk appeared in the doorway next to him. "Does it look any different? I don't think it looks any different."

Dave had been bailed. He had not been charged, which according to Fisk was a good thing, but the police investigation would continue. Fisk had driven them both back to HHHP Central, which was silent – devoid of both journalists and the party – and the campervan was nowhere to be seen. There was something sorrowful about the picture that greeted them – their spiritual home, lifeless and broken.

"I'll make some tea," said Dave, rummaging around for the kettle. "I need to hear what you know about this endowment though, Harry. You said it came through another law firm, right?"

Fisk nodded. "Yeah, Plumpton and Bradley. But I already tried them. Rang them, phoned them, faxed them – they're hiding behind professional privilege. But even if they weren't, they're not going to speak to us. If this money's bent, then they're up the chocolate-tunnel without a spoon as well, because they sent it on to you."

Dave found the kettle behind the sofa and ran it under the tap. "We need to find out who did this. I am *not* going to prison just because someone gave us some money. I didn't know it was stolen!"

Fisk shrugged. "Hey, look, if you're innocent –"

"I am! You bloody know I am!"

"– Then the cops will find out who really did it, and you'll be fine. Relax."

Dave was looking for the teapot. "Relax? *Relax?* I've been nicked for money laundering because of money *you* gave me, and you say relax? And where the hell is the teapot?"

Dave had never heard a gunshot before.

Sandport's violent crime problem revolved mostly around a belligerent seagull that would occasionally take over the dairy aisle of the local supermarket. The pigeons could be a bit problematic too, but mostly in a fluttery, gobbly sense that had yet to progress to firearms. Other than that, the only incident of note had been two years ago when an elderly lady on a motorised scooter had exceeded the speed limit and frightened a cat. And so, a low *pop* and the tinkling of glass did not immediately concern him.

"What was that?" he said.

"The window's broken," observed Fisk. "Was it broken before?"

There was another *pop*, this time accompanied by a thud as something slammed into the wall by Dave's head. Dave turned to inspect a hole that had appeared. He sniffed it. It smelled like fireworks.

"Bloody hell!" he shouted. "It's a gun! That's a gun! Get down!"

Dave dived behind the sofa, leaving Fisk standing by the window, frowning.

"Is it a gun? It sounds like popcorn."

"Harry, get the hell behind the sofa! It's a gun, it's a bloody gun!"

"Really? It didn't sound like a gun."

"What? Do you want to invite the bullet to climb back into the barrel and try to sound more gunny this time, or do you want to *get behind the sofa!*"

This time there was a succession of pops, and bullet-holes appeared across the wall behind them. Fisk yelped and dived behind the sofa with Dave.

"It's a gun!" whispered Fisk.

"Well, call the police then!"

"You call the police!"

"The police have got my phone!"

"Well, then! They'll be here any minute!"

"What?"

"Shh – listen!"

They fell silent. There were footsteps outside, on the road.

Then on the step.

Then in the room.

"Harry," whispered Dave.

"Yes?"

"I don't think it's the police."

The sofa roared as it was pulled back, and the cowering men found themselves staring up at an enormous, bald, umber-skinned man with a big, beaming smile. A smart, black suit and dark tie stretched across a broad chest. Dave's eyes drifted down the man's left arm, upon which scarcely-concealed biceps taunted equally swollen triceps, all the

way down to a gigantic hand that held a gleaming automatic
pistol.

The pistol had a long silencer on the end. Dave knew
about those from the movies.

"Hello," said Dave, as politely as possible. "Can we help
you?"

"Mr David Williams?" asked the man.

Fisk pointed at Dave. "He is! That one!"

The man's unblinking eyes settled on Dave.

"Is this true?" he said, raising the gun.

"Um," said Dave. "I – I genuinely can't remember."

"Mr Ubi and Mr Oba want to know where their
money is."

"What, um, what money would that be? Oh, no," said
Dave, trailing off as he felt the end of the silencer rest on his
forehead.

"You know what money, Mr David Williams. I am not a
patient man. I am very impervious."

"I – I think you mean impetuous," said Fisk.

The man looked at Fisk and smiled. "Oh! Thank you!
Yes, yes that is what I am. Impetuous."

"You're most welcome."

The man pointed at Fisk. "You know, you are a very
helpful and educated man. What is your profession?"

"I'm a lawyer," said Fisk, with considerably less gusto
than usual.

"A most noble occupation!" said the man. "Here, take my
card," he added, reaching inside his jacket pocket and
handing a business card to Fisk. "I do quite a bit of work for
lawyers. Actually, quite a bit of work *to* lawyers."

"Thank you," said Fisk, reading the card. It said, simply,
'The Panther'. "What, er, line of business, are you in?"

The Panther turned back to Dave, the forehead of whom the silenced gun had not left. "Disputes," he smiled.

"Look," said Dave. "We sort of spent it. And there's some left, but we can't get to it because the police have frozen our accounts."

"Well that is a shame," said the Panther. "Because now you are of no use, and I must direct my enquiries elsewhere. You may pray now."

Dave closed his eyes, grimaced, and waited for the inevitable.

And then, suddenly, the gun left Dave's forehead.

"What does impervious mean?" asked the Panther, turning back to Fisk and relaxing the gun.

"It means indestructible."

"Ah!" exploded the Panther. "I am that as well! Ha, ha!"

"Oh!" said Fisk. "Ha, ha! Ha, ha, ha!"

Abruptly, the Panther's face fell serious again, and he replaced the gun on Dave's forehead.

"Very funny. Mr Williams, to you, Mr Obi and Mr Uba say 'hello'."

"Oh, well – hi," said Dave.

He closed his eyes again, and swallowed, and just at the moment he expected oblivion to descend, there was a crash of china.

He looked up. The Panther blinked and, wordlessly, tumbled to the floor. Dillon stood over him, shards of china at his feet.

"Oh! *There's* the teapot!" exclaimed Dave.

8

"Dillon!" said Dave. "What are you doing here?"

They stood over the Panther's face-down, motionless form, which took up a considerable area of floor-space.

"I've been here for ages," replied Dillon. "I was only outside. But hey! You're out! Who's this guy?"

"He said his name was the Panther and he wanted to kill me," said Dave.

"He had very handsome business cards, though," said Fisk. "They were embossed, you know."

"Yes, thank you Harry," said Dave. "What the hell are we going to do with this? Is he breathing? Is he – dead?"

Dillon knelt down and put his cheek to the Panther's face. "No – he's breathing. He's just out cold."

"So, what now?"

"Okay," said Fisk. "Here's what we do. We get three shovels, five kilos of lime, and bleach; lots of bleach. We get it all from different hardware stores. We wait a few hours, and then – I know a place, not far from here."

There was a pause.

"Bury him?" said Dave. "That's the advice of the general counsel of the Happening Happy Hippy Party? He's not dead, Harry!"

Dillon stood up. "Well, we can't leave him here. The press could come back at any moment, and the headline will be 'HHHP in racist attack outrage'."

"We're not going to the police," said Dave, shaking his head. "They want to pin whatever they can on me. I don't trust them at all."

"Can't we just, you know, dump him somewhere?" said Dillon. "Maybe he'll wake up and think it was all a dream. Or have an epiphany about how a life of violence is an ultimately fruitless waste."

Dave leaned against the kitchen counter. "No, he'll just come back, like some horrid, murdery homing pigeon. Look, he was talking about Obi and Uba – they're the people that the police seem to think the money came from. So, he knows something. We could, you know – ask him."

Dillon nodded. "Let's take him to Green House. Riz closed it, it should be empty. We can use the campervan."

"Okay," said Fisk. "Here's what we do. We need a hosepipe, a towel, a reclining chair and some rope."

"What? We're not going to water-board him, Harry," said Dave. "Just – you know, gently restrain him, so that he doesn't blow my head off. Tie him up, maybe. For a bit. Not in a nasty way."

"How are we going to make sure that nobody sees him on the way? We need to put him in something," said Dillon.

"Okay," said Fisk. "Here's what we do –"

"No!" said Dave and Dillon.

"Hey, you don't know what I was going to say!"

"If it was anything other than 'wrap him in one of our

throws and claim he's furniture', we don't want to know,"
said Dillon.

"Oh yeah, yeah that probably would be better," said
Fisk. "Less chance of suffocation than my idea."

"Good."

"And less blood."

DUNCAN STARLING SAT at the bar in a Mayfair hotel, staring
at two items before him.

One was a phone, and the other was a tumbler of scotch.
Apart from bringing up the number of a police inspector
friend, which sat on the screen now, he had touched neither
since each had been placed there.

Aside from the patter of rain on the windows, the hotel
bar was quiet. In a corner somewhere behind, a fat, chuck-
ling Russian man of advancing age sat with a slender, young
woman. Whether she was being paid or not, she was doing a
relatively good job of behaving like she wanted to be there.
The barman, smartly dressed in a paisley waistcoat and
crisp white shirt, tended diligently to his duties. Starling sat
alone.

Distracting the media from the source of the HHHP's
funds had not been as difficult as he had anticipated. The
media largely distracted *themselves*. Crashing revenues had
turned it into an industry of ambulance-chasers. The big
names kept themselves afloat these days by churning out
copy-pasted press releases and mountains of intern-
harvested clickbait. The remnant of real investigative journalists were easily kept busy with a steady drip of seedy
stories about Opposition politicians, and those perfect civil

service scandals that were salacious enough to be interesting, but inconsequential enough to be forgotten.

Starling's police friend was a good chap. Honest and sensible, low-paid and insignificant. It was hard to be the former but not the latter – Starling made his own choice a while ago. And now, he had spent more than an hour sitting here, contemplating whether to call him. To do whatever the jargon was now. Whistle-blow. Make a disclosure. Come clean, put an end to this sorry mess.

It was thinking about his mother than had done it. The activist, the ethicist, the force in his life that told him he could change the world. And he had, hadn't he? He'd got this lot elected – with their promises, and smiles, and calm, steady hands. That had been the right thing to do. He hadn't known that they would turn to the dark side, had he?

He picked up the glass of scotch, and examined the twinkling glass, the amber shimmering through the faux crystal.

Yes, he sighed inwardly, replacing it on the bar. He'd known. Of course he'd known. They all do. Westminster was like a jungle; anything near it for too long was eventually consumed. The vines, and the tendrils, and the ferns wrap around it slowly – oh, so slowly – and then you look back, and all that's there is jungle. Dark, sinister jungle and a dark, sinister Prime Minister.

Starling glanced at the phone.

He'd lose his job, if he did it. And maybe never work again – nobody trusts a whistle-blower, not really. He could write some memoires maybe, get a few royalties from that – but nobody outside of Westminster really read those anyway. Maybe do a reality TV show. Or just embrace unemployment, spend all day in his pants, eat jam straight from the jar.

He shuddered. That would mean spending more time with Mrs Starling.

Could he even go to prison? Probably. He was part of it, after all. Despite his party's insistence in opposition that prisons were like holiday resorts, he knew that to be completely untrue. Prisons were *awful*. He'd heard that they re-use the teabags.

And then there was the money. One of prison's defining characteristics was the poor benefits package. It would mean pulling his two teenage children out of their private school, Horton Park. That would be the end of their first-rate education, school trips to Val d'Isère and work experience at investment banks. They'd have to go to the local state school, with its school trips to the local bread factory and work experience at Argos. Horton Park had recently introduced augmented reality teaching suites in the science department. The only augmented reality they'd get at the state school was ketamine in the playground.

So, they would suffer, right? His children, his family. If he blew the whistle? Yes, of course they would. Goodbye, London townhouse, stability and security. Hello, terraced property in Romford and worrying about how the kids' new friends had offensive tattoos and vacant stares. No – he couldn't do it. Not for him, of course, but for them. For the children.

Starling nodded to himself. That seemed like the right decision. He picked up the phone, clicked it off and slipped it into his jacket pocket. With a new surge of purpose, he pushed the whisky away and left a twenty-pound note for the barman. There would be no phone calls today.

And then, as he left his bar stool and walked to the door, a thought crawled across Duncan Starling's mind. A thought that he, too, had been consumed by the jungle. But this time, he did not nod. He simply pulled his coat tightly around himself, and the dark, sinister director of communications stepped out into the rain.

MARTHA PULLED up her Mini outside a small, terraced house and turned off the engine.

"Okay," said Catie, unclicking her seatbelt and opening the passenger door. "Paul's the executive director of the FCU. If we can get him onside, then I've got no doubt that all their whizzy tech will find the link we need."

"I hope so," replied Martha, as they left the car and walked up to the front door. Catie knocked.

After a pause, it opened, and the warm, orangey glow of a night-in flooded out onto the street. Paul, slightly tubby and bespectacled, stood in the doorway in a t-shirt and shorts, a glass of wine in hand and the sound of the television wafting over his shoulders from the front room.

"Catie, hi," said Paul, blinking. "What's going on? How are Dave and Rufus? What's happening?"

"Hi Paul," said Catie. "Rufus is out on bail. I don't know about Dave yet. But we need your help."

Paul glanced at Martha. "How, er, how can I help?"

"This is Martha Lewandowski, from the *Chronicle*," said Catie. "She has information that Winstanley Mortimer may be connected to the Prime Minister. We need the FCU to explore that possibility, chase down whatever the link is. There might be something big here, and something that could help to show that Dave and Rufus are innocent. This could be corruption on an intergalactic level, Paul."

Paul nodded as she spoke, adding an occasional 'mm' of

agreement. "Yeah," he said finally. "We're not going to be able to do that."

Catie balked. "Well, that's very surprising, Paul."

"No, it's not 'very surprising'," said Paul. "It's not 'very surprising' at all. 'Very surprising' would be if you ordered a takeaway pizza and when you got it home, it crawled out of the box and ate the cat. That would be 'very surprising'. What this is, is very *not* surprising. In fact, I would call this 'very predictable'."

"There's no need to be –"

"The FCU is an independent organisation, and you're straight-up asking us to do something partisan. This is the undue influence of our sinister corporate overlords."

Catie shrugged. "I'm not sure that the Happening Happy Hippy Party has ever been described as 'sinister corporate overlords'. Come on, Paul, this is totally within your remit and totally legit. This is breaking news. We're just asking you to fact-check the story before it's published."

"I will not allow my analysts to be used to serve private interests!"

"You used them to look up that ex-boyfriend," called out Paul's husband from the sofa.

"Yes, thank you Steve," snapped Paul.

"You're most welcome," replied Steve, through a mouth full of popcorn.

"*Really*," said Martha.

"That was a training exercise!" said Paul.

"I think that sounds like a major breach of FCU policy, at a very senior level, Catie. What do you think?" asked Martha.

Catie's eyes didn't leave Paul. "I agree, Martha. Very serious."

Paul sighed. "Come by the office first thing in the morning."

AMY SAT on a bench by Seahaven's small harbour, looking out at the sea beyond the masts and wheelhouses that bobbed against the night sky. Apart from the distant sound of the waves against the sea wall, the moonlit scene before her was silent. The gulls had disappeared to wherever gulls go, and only the occasional bark of a dog rose above the town to interfere with her thoughts.

She didn't know why she had come to Seahaven. The extent of her plan had been to get in her car, point it north, and drive until she ran out of petrol or hit a coastline. Somewhere after Manchester she had started seeing signs for Seahaven, and it reminded her of a happier time. It had seemed so idyllic, so peaceful when she had been putting together the campaign tour. So, she left the motorway, and when she arrived had parked up by the boats.

That was hours ago. She had barely moved from the bench since, except to buy chips. Her mind told her she needed food, but her body had refused to touch them. The seagulls had taken advantage of the situation.

Somewhere inside was a strange sort of anger. Indignation, even; she had agreed to help game a bunch of no-hoper wannabes. That was not what the Happening Happy Hippy Party had turned out to be. It was the real thing. People you could believe in, trust in. That wasn't part of the agreement, it wasn't fair that she had come to believe in them and trust them. It wasn't fair that she had realised she *was* them.

And Dave. The man who seemed so silly at first, but

developed so rapidly – who showed such fire, such commitment. The man who made her feel hope again, about
government, about society. The man she wanted to kiss, but
was employed to betray. Did she love him? Did that matter?

Amy sniffed. It was all lies, of course. Rationalisation.
She had fallen in love with a party and with a man – both of
whom had trusted her, and to both of whom she had been
lying from the first moment they met. She was Judas,
Edward Pevensie, Brutus. Gollum. She was a device of the
system they fought. She *was* the system.

"Evening, love," said a voice, and she looked up.

A police officer stood by the bench, his face lit in a
strange yellow above his high-visibility body armour and
chirping radio. He smiled.

"Oh," she said. "Hi, I'm sorry, I'm just – is there a problem?"

"Not at all," said the officer. "May I join you?"

Amy gestured to the bench. "Be my guest. I'm not much
conversation though."

The officer eased himself down onto the bench. "Don't
think anyone is at this time of night, love."

As he sat, she noticed that he had long, grey hair tied
behind his head. She also noticed he was holding a flask,
the cap of which he unscrewed and set down gently on the
bench. He poured steamy coffee into it, and offered it to her.

"Thank you," she said, gladly wrapping her hands
around the warmth and taking in the aroma.

"You're most welcome. It's a cold night to be sitting out
enjoying the view."

She sipped the coffee and looked at him. "I'm sorry," she
said. "You don't often see police officers with long hair."

The officer smiled and gestured to an epaulette, which
bore the silver 'SC' of the Special Constabulary – the volun-

teer police. "Just doing my bit," he said. "I find there is a real inner peace in serving the community in different ways, don't you? I'm Michael, delighted to meet you."

Amy shook his outstretched hand. "Amy," she said.

Michael produced another small cup from somewhere and poured himself some coffee. "We are very blessed, here," he said. "Such a beautiful view, such a beautiful community. A good place to come to escape. It's important to care for those who need to check out of the world for a moment."

Amy shrugged and pulled her coat tighter around her.

Michael reached into a utility pouch and unfolded a foil blanket. "I'm sorry I don't have anything more fashionable," he said, wrapping it around her.

"Thank you," Amy smiled weakly.

They sat in silence for a short while, sipping the coffee. Amy wasn't sure what it was – the kindness or the company, but the final dike burst and tears began to drip down her cheeks.

"I'm sorry," she said, wiping them away with her sleeve. "I don't do tears."

Michael offered her a tissue. "We all do tears, love."

"I just – I don't even know how to describe it. I don't know how to think about it. I thought I was doing the right thing. But I was lying to everyone, including me, and it turned out that it was the wrong thing – and the right thing was in front of me the whole time, and now I've let it be destroyed. Now all there is, is wrongness."

Michael didn't speak for a moment, and took another sip of coffee.

"I had a dog once," he said, eventually. "Archie, he was called. He was a great dog."

Amy didn't say anything. She was too tired to challenge the segue.

"Huge great golden retriever, Archie. Long, glossy coat. Great temperament. We had this silly rubber bone thing, and all he really loved was catching that little rubber bone when I threw it, and bringing it back to me. Golden retriever, eh? I suppose the clue's in his name."

Michael took a sip of coffee.

"So, one afternoon, we're out on our walk, and we're by a pond. And I'm throwing the bone, and Archie's catching it. And then I throw it this one time, and it goes flying off to the bank of the pond. And as Archie goes charging after it, we both realise there's a child splashing in the water. Not a good splashing, Amy. I don't know how the boy got there, but he didn't have any time left. His head was going under. And, you know, Archie *saw him*. In those moments, I saw Archie look between his bone, and the boy, and there was confusion there. Archie was caught between the bone, and the boy."

Michael turned to Amy and smiled.

"Sometimes, when we're chasing our rubber bone, we encounter something important. And we have a choice to make, and not very long to make it. Do we stick with our bone?"

Amy looked back. "What did Archie choose?"

Michael shrugged. "What do you think he chose?"

"Did he choose the boy?"

"Yes, he did. He jumped into the water and grabbed the boy's shirt and pulled him out. He got an award you know. But he fought his instincts to do so."

There was silence for a moment.

"Hope is precious, Amy. When we're called to steward it, it's almost always a surprise. But it's always important."

Amy looked away, and then turned back a moment later. "Should I go back?"

"I find that if we are honest, then we already know the answers to questions like that."

Amy nodded, and stood up. "I think I need to go back."

THE CAMPERVAN TRUNDLED through the dark, empty streets of Sandport. Dillon sat at the wheel, Dave nervously beside him. Fisk lurked in the back, next to a roll of carpet that looked remarkably like it contained a person.

"You didn't have to take his clothes off," said Dave.

"Sure I did, Davey!" said Fisk. "Helps stop him escaping!"

"One minute he's a lawyer, the next he's in *Grand Theft Auto*," murmured Dillon.

"You sound very chipper, Harry," said Dave. "Considering the circumstances."

"I love this," said Fisk, sitting back against the bulkhead. "Reminds me of Iraq. Wish I had a cigar."

Dillon rolled his eyes. "You weren't in Iraq, Harry."

"Sure. I mean, like, the movies."

Dave turned around. "In which Iraq movie did someone get knocked out with a teapot, wrapped in a rug and driven off in a van with a deranged lawyer that took his clothes?"

"Oh," said Fisk. "Trivia, love this. Okay, let me think; not *Jarhead*, that was Gyllenhaal –"

"Um, Dave," said Dillon. "What do we do if there are loads of people at Green House?"

"It's nearly two in the morning, and you said it yourself – it's locked up. Nobody's going to be there."

"Sure. Probably. Who are these guys, then?"

Dave looked up. The square outside Green House was full. Protesters stretched as far as the eye could see, some with tents and campervans. Placards sprouted up from the crowd, bearing legends like 'first they came for the Hippies', 'we want more HH-HP sauce', and 'je suis Dave'. Most, however, simply stormed 'they're innocent'.

Dave's mouth dropped open as his eyes roamed across woolly-hatted protesters of all ages, shapes and sizes warming their hands over braziers and singing together over candles. Something powerful seemed to strike him in his chest, something like relief, hope and love encountered each other in the sauna of a twenty-four gym and got to chatting. He felt tears begin to threaten.

As the campervan pulled into the square, a wave of recognition swept over the camp, and protesters surged towards them.

"It's beautiful," said Dave, as the crowd embraced the van, waving at them with broad smiles.

"It is very kind, yes," said Dillon. "They will, of course, be less pleased to see us when they find a half-naked, captive African fellow in the back."

Fisk's face appeared behind their shoulder. "Shit!" he said. "This is pretty frickin' inconvenient if you're trying to smuggle in a body!"

"He's not a body, Harry!" said Dave.

Dillon was rolling down a window. "I'll think of something. Hi!"

"Hi!" said the girl closest to the window. "It's so good to see you!"

"You too!" beamed Dillon, with perhaps just a little too much enthusiasm. "What – what's happening here?"

"It's a vigil!" said the girl. "We knew you'd come back!"

"That's great! Who are you guys?" asked Dillon.

"We're staffers," she said, indicating to several young people around her, who all waved and smiled. "I'm Jo! That's Rachel and Tina, they're in fundraising. This is Bradley, he's in the call centre. That's Jon from campaign co-ordination! Hi Jon!"

Jon waved.

"Hi Jon," said Dillon, with an anaemic wave. "All these people are campaign staff?"

"Oh no!" said Jo. "We just started it, then other party members joined in, then anti-fascist people, then the public, and it just sort of grew from there! The camp goes all the way to the post office! The media are here with their cameras, you know! We knew you'd come back to get the campaign going, we're ready to go back to work! We can still win!"

"The media are here with their cameras! Brilliant! Okay, well, we'll just drive round the back and then unlock the doors from inside, and we can all get to work!"

Jo cocked her head. "From the inside? You can just unlock them from the outside, here! You can see the lock, there!"

"Yes, but, you know, reasons. Okay, bye Jo!"

Dillon hastily rolled up the window and began reversing.

"Smooth," said Dave. "Reasons."

"Just pray I don't manage to knock anybody over," murmured Dillon, concentrating on the mirrors as he turned the van round. "One body is inconvenient, two is careless."

"Harry, give me your phone," said Dave. "We need to get Riz in. Someone needs to organise these guys."

The crowd parted, and Dillon drove the campervan to the service access at the back of the building. Quickly, in case they were followed, they hauled the bulging carpet out of the back and into Green House.

STARLING'S RINGTONE jolted him from his sleep only a second or two before he knew what it was, which in turn was a second or two before his hand knew that his brain had filed a request for it to leave the bed.

"Hello, Prime Minister," said Starling, slamming the phone to his head. It rang again, and he realised he hadn't actually answered it.

Starling sat up, poked the screen and cleared his throat. "Hello, Prime Minister," he said.

"Duncan! Have you seen the bloody telly?"

Starling rubbed his face, turned on a bedside lamp and reached over to Mrs Starling's side for the television remote. She was staying at her sister's. Well, apparently. She seemed to have been there a while.

"Any particular channel, sir?"

"All of them!" barked the Prime Minister. "All the bloody channels!"

Starling's TV burst into life, on the channel he'd seen last - a foreign-owned, twenty-four hour news channel. They were like the British ones, only angrier. The screen filled with images of a huge candlelit demonstration.

"Oh yeah," said Starling, rubbing his eyes. "It's the HHHP protest. There's a load of people outside their head-quarters."

"Well, why?" snapped the Prime Minister.

"They don't believe it," said Starling. "They don't trust the establishment, they think it's all a set-up."

"Pah! Set-up indeed – there's no trust for institutions or authority anymore!"

Starling shrugged. "But, it *is* a set-up, sir."

"Yes, but they don't know that," said the Prime Minister, testily. "Keep up, Duncan!"

Starling swung his feet out of bed and willed his body to stand up. "Well, Sandport is something we haven't talked about, sir. The HHHP were way out in front, there – only BEEF came a close second. There's a very real risk – even a probability – that BEEF is going to win it now."

"Why the hell should I care about that? Are we winning the election or not?"

"Well – yes sir."

"Then why should I give a damn if a bunch of loony fascists win a seat?"

"Because it'll be the thin end of the wedge. It'll help to legitimise them. They're already on about five percent nationally, that's unheard of in –"

"Why are you wasting my time with this claptrap, Duncan? I couldn't give a pensioner's skidmark whether Excruciating Thorne is in parliament, prison or bloody outer space. If a town of unemployed, window-licking, elbow-biting, excuse-me-doc-could-you-take-a-look-at-my-unusual-facial-rash, charity-shopping, walking dead wanted to elect a decomposing, week-old, crispy dog turd as their MP I wouldn't give a damn, so tell me why I should care if they want to elect a breathing one?"

"Sir, you can't ignore the far-right, their narrative is catching on worldwide. We need to –"

"Oh, do we, Duncan? Do *we*? Let me remind you who the bloody Prime Minister is, Duncan! Who is it? Hang on, I think I know this one – yes, yes it's me, I think? Is it me?"

"Yes, Prime Minister."

"It *is* bloody me! Good bloody night!"

The Prime Minister hung up, and Starling looked down at his phone and sighed.

"Well," he said. "You've taken half their policies, so maybe you'll just plagiarise them into oblivion."

THE PANTHER SAT on an office chair in only his boxer shorts and socks, an electrical cable wrapped tightly around his impressive muscles and his powerful hands secured behind him.

They had put him in Catie's office, as it was closer to the stairwell and therefore the easiest to which to carry him. Blinds had been pulled down over the internal windows to conceal him from the staffers, and Harry had been sent off to organise the masses with Riz, who had recommended a colossal doorstep campaign in the morning, the last day before the election. Dave had been too tired to disagree.

Blearily, the Panther began to stir.

"What – what is, where is?" He mumbled, looking down at the cables and trying to move his hands.

Dave, who had been lying on a couch, sat up. "He's awake!" he whispered. "What do we do now?"

Dillon, sitting on Catie's desk, shrugged. "Wing it," he whispered. "You know, encourage him to talk to us."

Dave cleared his throat. "Well, hello again, Mr Panther."

The Panther blinked a few times, and looked up.

"You," he said. "David Williams. You have done this."

"It's no use trying to free yourself, Mr Panther, you are quite convincingly secured."

The Panther looked up at Dave with the dead, soulless eyes of a shark. "Perhaps I have underestimated you, David

Williams," he said, slowly. "Perhaps you are more serious than I thought."

"Yeah," nodded Dave. "Yeah, I'm serious. You didn't know who you were messing with, right?"

"You must forgive me, David Williams. It can be difficult to recognise the godfathers of another country. I knew you were a political leader, yes, but I did not know you were – serious."

Dave glanced at Dillon, and then with a puffed-out chest turned back to the Panther. "I understand," he said, as authoritatively as he could. "You can repent of your disrespect by providing information, Mr Panth –"

"Once before, I made this mistake," said the Panther, apparently ignoring him. "I underestimated Monsieur Papa Diop, whom I took for a regular businessman. This was because he was a small, friendly man, of whom nobody spoke ill. I could find no trace that he was serious – no rumours, no bodies. But when I entered his residence, he had men, and I was shot."

The Panther nodded to a gnarl of damaged skin on his arm.

"I was bound and dropped into the Gambia, and left for dead, and Monsieur Diop was able to escape. But I swam, and survived, and resumed my mission. It was some time before I was able to catch up with Monsieur Diop, at a wedding in Dubai. I took the opportunity to cut his throat during the celebrations, and those of his daughters, and then I burned down the wedding reception. Many died. But men like you and I, David Williams, we understand this game, yes? We understand these rules. As did, I expect, Monsieur Diop."

There was a pause.

"Um," said Dave. "I, er, well I'm not that serious –"

"You may do your worst," said the Panther. "I will not tell you what you wish to know. You are not the first serious man to torture me."

"Dave, can I have a word?" asked Dillon, and beckoned him to the corner.

"What the hell are we going to do with this guy?" whispered Dave. "I feel like we've captured a robot killing machine from the future. If he gets out of that cable – which I might remind you, comes from Catie's TV and is not guaranteed for use in restraining international hit-men – he's going to lay waste to this entire building."

"There can be no pain to which you may introduce me," said the Panther's voice. "I know all the pains. You will only reacquaint me. When you apply hot irons to my feet I will say, 'hello, old friend'. When you push blades under my fingernails, I will greet them with the warmth of an elderly relative. When you hit me with a club, I will say 'beautiful club, how I missed you, let us make the angry love'. When you –"

Dillon leaned in to Dave. "Look, you need to be fresh for tomorrow – the Sandport Decides event is key now. That's our last chance to stop BEEF winning on Thursday."

Dave blinked in surprise. "You think we should still fight the election? Even with all this?"

"Of course," said Dillon. "More now than ever. Go and get some sleep, I'll sit with him. Talk to him."

There was a tap at the door. Dave strode over and opened it slightly.

"Yes?" he said.

It was Jo, with a big smile and a tray of coffee cups. "Hi Dave! We thought maybe you guys needed refreshment."

"No thanks Jo," replied Dave, affecting Dillon's over-enthusiasm from earlier. "We're good!"

"Nonsense!" beamed Jo, pushing her way through the door. "You need sustenance! And maybe hugs, hugs for everyone – you need to know what we're with you! I'll put these down and we'll do hugs!"

As the door moved slightly further ajar, Jo's eyes bulged at the scene over Dave's shoulder. "Oh golly. Wow, um. What, who is –"

Dillon appeared behind Dave, blocking the view and ushering Jo back into the main office. "It's a sex thing," he said.

"A sex – thing?"

"Yeah," said Dillon. "It's been a traumatic day, we just need to relax."

"I am the Panther!" shouted the Panther.

"Okay, thanks, bye," went on Dillon, closing the door to Jo's alarmed face.

Dave sighed. "Sex thing," he repeated. "That's the best you could come up with?"

"Your plan to use sexual torture will fail," went on the Panther, with grim stoicism. "It will not be the first time that acts of depravity have been metered out to me. But as Mr Emmanuel Sesay learned after he dressed me like a lady, and applied the clamps, the rubber pole and the goat, the only boundary to depravity is the extent of one's creativity, and I will always –"

"Oh my goodness, make him stop," said Dave.

THE SUN ROSE over Sandport on the final day of the campaign, a town whose divisions were marked out by the political placards that dotted its windows and gardens.

The blue, red and yellow signs of the major parties had

become a rarity. Those that did remain stood proud over hedgerows that twinkled in the frost of the spring morning. The red and black of BEEF's had shrunk over the weeks as the orange of the HHHP had advanced, but overnight, much of that orange had been eclipsed by graffiti. Fresh, guerrilla red and black had appeared mysteriously on walls and across shop-fronts – especially those owned by people who seemed to belong to one minority or another.

From the warmth of the Mercedes' front passenger seat, Alicia Rhodes watched Excelsior Thorne step out of his house into the crisp, May air and a throng of waiting TV cameras and camera flashes. At the end of his garden path, police officers restrained rival groups of BEEF supporters and anti-fascist protesters who screamed and chanted at each other as much as Thorne. Her phone was streaming one of the live news channels, so even from the comfort of the car she could hear the storm outside.

"Do you really think you will win tomorrow?" asked a journalist as the force of Thorne's stride parted their cluster, a broad – and genuine – smile across his face.

"What do you have to say to accusations that you are fostering racism here, Mr Thorne?" shouted another, over the canopy of boom mics.

"Do you condemn the wave of homophobic graffiti appearing in schools across the constituency, Mr Thorne?"

"Excelsior, over here - what do you have to say about the attack on a group of Turkish workers last night?"

Several heavy-set BEEF staffers protected Thorne from the press, the faux-gentility of their tweed suits and flat caps betrayed by hipster haircuts, shaved heads or the tips of racist tattoos visible at their necklines. One opened the door for him to climb into the Mercedes.

For a moment, Alicia noted the anger of the BEEF

supporters and the fear of the protesters. Then she wondered if the emotions were, in fact, the same. Who was afraid of whom? And how different were all these people, really? Was this the unity BEEF declared that they would bring, or was this a deepened, scarring division?

For a second – just a second – Alicia Rhodes detected a short, uneasy footnote at the page of her mind that maybe something wasn't quite right here.

"Good morning, team," said Thorne, stepping into the car as a staffer closed the door behind him. "Are we ready to make history?"

Bart, sitting in the back, shook Thorne's hand. "Congratulations, Ex – you're nearly BEEF's first MP."

"Keep the foot on the gas for another twenty-four hours, and the seat's yours," said Alicia. "So, a refresh on this morning's itinerary – we'll go to the BEEF campaign office where we have some press meetings lined up, and then on to Sandport Decides."

"Good. Any word from the Hopeless Halfwit Hand-job Party?"

Bart grinned. "Not a peep, and the online chatter isn't kind to them."

"Good," snorted Thorne. "What are we waiting for? Let's go."

A tweed-suited staffer sat at the wheel, but the protesters blocked the road in front. "Could have trouble here, boss," he said.

"Just run them the hell over," said Bart. "Seriously. Just start driving. If they don't get out of the way, that's natural selection."

Alicia glanced behind her at Bart, who stared back in defiance.

"Hey! If you're going to make an omelette, the eggs are going to complain, right?"

DAVE DID NOT KNOW where he was.

There was just darkness, inky darkness, all around him. It was so complete, and so abundant, that he could not tell where the darkness ended, and he began. Was he underground? Inside? Outside? Was it night? No – even the night had never been as dark as this. Nothing Dave had ever known had been as dark as this.

"Hello?" he said, his voice swallowed by the silent blackness.

There was nothing, for a moment, and he was alone with his thoughts. And then, suddenly, there was something else.

"You've been a very naughty boy, David," said a familiar voice. "What am I to do with you?"

Dave looked up, panic rising inside him like vomit. He thought that perhaps he could see a figure – someone present, but unmoving, cloaked in the black. And then, through the gloom, he thought he could make out the faint, bluish outline of a crown – and the scent of carnations.

"Your Majesty?"

Dave opened his eyes and squinted, sunshine streaming across his face. He was lying on a sofa in a break-out area at Green House, and it wasn't so much the sun that woke up him – but the sound of a fully-operational, fully-engaged political campaign around him.

Activists were packing bags of leaflets and dealing out handsome, orange rosettes. Talking points had been scrawled up on whiteboards. Teams were being briefed.

Phones rang – but only momentarily, answered immediately by smiling staffers.

Riz and Rufus stood over Dave.

"Morning Dave," said Riz, handing him a cup of coffee.

Dave sat up, rubbed his eyes and took the coffee gratefully. "Riz, Rufus, hi – wow, this is great."

"It was pushing at an open door, really. All these guys were outside, wanting to go back to work. All Harry and I did really was just get them back at their desks. Sure, there are hardly any computers in the building now but, do we need them? There's going to be a massive doorstep campaign today – not just here, but nationwide, and a big phone bank too. Everybody's going to be out on the streets or on the wires, except those who are going to Sandport Decides to support you."

Dave sipped the coffee. "And where is Harry now?"

Riz smiled, and stepped aside so that Dave could see Harry sprawled across a big, pink beanbag, snoring loudly. "He didn't last long," he said.

"And Amy?" asked Dave, standing up. "Anything?"

Rufus shook his head. "I'm sorry."

Dave finished the coffee. "Well, that's that, I guess. So, the plan is to do Sandport Decides, hit the streets, and hope for the best?"

Riz nodded. "More than hope for the best. The latest indications are that we've lost a lot of our swing voters – but that we've generated our own core voters, and those guys think what happened yesterday is an establishment set-up."

"It was," said Dave.

"Can't fool the electorate," shrugged Riz. "But the question now is – how many voters were swing, and how many were core? So while we try to swing as many back as we can, the other aim for today is to ensure none from the latter slip to the former. And we're going to focus on Sandport – we're bringing in activists from the neighbouring constituencies. At this stage, how well we do nationally is a big uncertainty – but we definitely need to stop BEEF here."

"Agreed. What time are people setting off?"

"Nine. It might be good if you spoke to them – said a few words. Encourage them? I think they would like to see you."

Dave checked his watch. "Done. Have them all here on the main office floor at five to nine. I need to wash up and sort something out."

Riz nodded, patted Dave's shoulder and headed back into the throng of staffers. Dave and Rufus weaved between the desks towards Catie's office.

"Did you get much sleep, at least?" asked Dave.

"Oh yeah, great night," said Rufus. "Dead to the world. Had dreams, you know. There was this giant killer bat, and then night came so it took flight to find things to kill, but there was this butterfly that came out of nowhere and bit its head off."

"That's, er, one for the dream-diary there, Rufus."

They arrived at Catie's office and Dave opened the door – and stared at the scene before him. Dillon and the Panther both sat cross-legged on the floor in their underpants. The television cabling lay neatly coiled beside the Panther.

"Yes!" the Panther was affirming, his eyes intense and his gestures forceful. "That is most insightful! For to replace neoliberalism, the alternative must be conversant with it - so that it can subvert it!"

Dillon gently spiked the air with his finger. "Exactly. Like a virus."

"Just like a virus! And this is why love is important, because it is inherent, it is already inside everybody! Not the sentimentality of the movies, the narrative we are sold, but the collection of actual behaviours and thoughts that consti-tute love! It is the soundest basis for all human endeavour! We must only operationalise what already exists inside everybody!"

Dillon smiled and nodded. "You've got it."

"You are a man of great wisdom," said the Panther. "Great wisdom!"

"Ahem," coughed Dave.

The Panther looked up, and pointed at Dillon. "This is a man of great wisdom!"

"Dillon," said Dave, slowly, as he edged into the room. "What is going on here?"

The Panther stood and bowed. "Mr David Williams, you are most fortunate that such a learned man is your advisor. He has explained everything to me!"

"The Panther has joined the party," said Dillon, waving an application form. "Turns out his real name is Philip."

"You've – converted an international hit-man to the Happening Happy Hippy Party?"

"Mr David Williams," said the Panther. "I am so fortu-nate to have met you. I think that maybe this is fate, yes? And I would have killed you! What would that have achieved? Pastor Dillon has explained the corrosive myth of redemptive violence!"

"*Pastor* Dillon?" echoed Rufus.

"Pastor Dillon, you – you seem to have removed your clothes, too," said Dave.

Dillon shrugged. "It felt right. You know, in the moment."

"Mr David Williams –"

"You only need to call me Dave, Philip."

"Of course! I am most humbled. Mr David Williams, please feel free for you both also to undress. It is liberating!"

"I'm game," said Rufus, unbuttoning his shirt.

"No, stop, can everybody stop taking off their clothes, please," said Dave, rubbing his temples. "I have only slept for a couple of hours and I am not completely sure that any of this is real, and the last thing I want to dream about is Rufus in the nip. You were supposed to interrogate the Panther and now –"

"Interrogate?" said Catie's voice, and Dave turned around to see Catie and Martha in the doorway. Catie's eyes were roaming across the naked bodies and cabling. "What – what the hell is going on in here?"

Dave shrugged. "I've really rather lost track," he said.

Dillon grunted as he rose to his feet. "Catie, meet Philip. Philip, meet Catie. Catie is our director of communications. Philip is an international contract killer who was hired by sinister African interests to murder Dave and retrieve Winstanley Mortimer's money. Fortunately, just as he was about to do so, I broke a teapot on his head – sorry about that, by the way."

The Panther shook his head. "No, you are most welcome, it was a necessary step in my transformation!"

"While he was out cold, we brought him here, tied him up with your TV cable, and were going to ask him who hired him and stuff. But instead I thought we'd have a lovely chat about the HHHP, and now he's renounced his life of violence and signed up."

Catie blinked. "I literally left you guys alone for, like, one evening."

Dillon gestured to Martha. "So, that's our new friend. Who's yours?"

"Hi," said Martha. "I'm Martha Lewandowski, *Sandport Chronicle*."

"She's a journalist?" said Dave. "You brought a journalist *here*?"

"Well, I didn't know you're turned my office into a bloody CIA black site! What were you thinking, tying up some guy with the TV cable?"

"I seem to have missed quite a lot," said Rufus.

"Oh," said Dillon, eyes wide in recognition and bobbing his head at Catie. "*This* is Martha? *The* Martha?"

"Yes," replied Martha with a quizzical frown. "You – know me?"

"Anyway," said Catie, rapidly. "We have news. *Big* news. Well, it was big until the – murder thing."

"So – what is it?" asked Dave.

"The Prime Minister knew Winstanley Mortimer," said Catie. "Martha says he was seen at the grave, paying his respects."

"What, really?" said Dave.

Dillon climbed onto one of the desks and resumed his cross-legged posture. "That's it?"

"I think that's pretty big," replied Martha. "Don't you?"

"Well – I'm just not sure it's all that surprising, I mean, Mortimer was super-rich, right? These guys move in the same kinds of circles."

"It's a fair point," said Martha. "Except that there is *nobody else* in Winstanley Mortimer's circle. The guy's a ghost."

"We're just on our way to the FCU," went on Catie. "See what they can dig up."

"Maybe Philip has something we can research," said Dave.

"Of course," said the Panther. "I renounce my life of futile hate and embrace your ideals of love and compassion. How may I help this most noble cause?"

"You can tell us why you came here," said Dave. "And how you came to start shooting at me."

The Panther nodded. "I was sent to retrieve Mr Ubi and Mr Oba's money, and indeed to kill you, Mr David Williams," said the Panther. "I was despatched by Mr Okoro, the executor to Mr Ubi and Mr Oba."

Dave folded his arms. "But why did Ubi and Oba give the money to Winstanley Mortimer in the first place?"

The Panther frowned. "I do not know who that is. The money was transmitted via an intermediary, Mr Ryan Callaghan. I met him once."

"Then what was it for? What were Mr Ubi and Mr Oba buying?"

"It was, I believe, a business deal – it was for permits. Clearances of some kind."

"*Ten million* for permits?" said Catie.

"Sometimes a very senior level of approval is required," shrugged the Panther.

Martha sat down at one of the desks. "What kind of business are Mr Uba and Mr Oba in, Philip?"

"Oh, they are in many businesses, Miss Martha. Financial services, hospitality, import-export, mining, transportation, infrastructure, healthcare, construction –"

Martha had found a pen and was writing at a pad. "Go on."

"Drug importation, human trafficking, the diversion of aid, illicit diamonds, extortion, bribery – many businesses. They are most important men."

"Where do they operate, Philip?"

"All over the world, Miss Martha. But they are based in Kundunga, in West Africa."

"Where there's a civil war," murmured Martha as she wrote.

"A most bloody and disastrous affair," said the Panther. And then added, sadly, "but very profitable, for those able to see opportunity in such a thing."

"So, do you know about any connection between Obi and Uba, Winstanley Mortimer, and the British Prime Minister?"

The Panther bowed his head. "I am sorry. I do not."

"Okay," said Catie. "Thank you, Philip. We'll take all this to the FCU and see what they can do. Dave – you need to be getting ready. You smell weird. Sandport Decides is starting soon and you need to be at your best."

"We need to stop Excelsior Thorne," agreed Dillon.

"I can kill him," said the Panther. "It will be easy. I will sneak past the security at this event, and slit his throat from behind. I will be gone before the first drops of blood begin to pool at his feet."

There was a silence, and the HHHP leadership looked awkwardly at each other.

The Panther laughed; a big, booming guffaw. "Your faces! I am joking! I renounce the violence of my past! Perhaps I will become a comedian, now, yes?"

"Baby steps, Philip, baby steps," said Dillon, as he stood up.

"Okay, team," said Dave, checking his watch. "I'm going to speak to the guys before they hit the streets, get a shower and do Sandport Decides. Catie and Martha, you get to the FCU. Rufus and Dillon, you're with me at the event. Philip – hang on, where's your gun?"

"Harry Fisk has it," said Dillon.

"Of course he does."

There was a knock at the door, and Riz appeared. "Dave, everybody's ready to go."

"Okay, let's do it," replied Dave, and followed Dave out onto the office floor.

As Dave left the office, he looked up to see the whole floor crammed with activists. Some stood on desks to get a better view, those closest to him had hit the floor. They were a rainbow, thought Dave – every ethnicity, every faith, every sexuality; male and female and everything in between. Hijabs and kippas, tattoos and tie-dye, youthful complexions and well-worn skin. They squeezed shoulder to shoulder, and erupted in a deafening cheer as Dave appeared.

Dave beamed, and raised his hands as the cheer subsided. "Good morning, everyone," he said.

"Good morning Dave!" replied the rainbow, in unison, and then cheered and laughed at their own eerie concord.

"It's been a hell of a twenty-four hours," said Dave. "But I want to thank you for your sincerity, and your commitment, and your trust. This party is about more than us. And you refused to believe that the lie, the plot that is afoot, is strong enough to stop that. To stop what we are about, who we are, and the job we need to do now."

Dave pointed to the window. "Everything has changed out there, and this country is facing a choice. What does it believe in? What does it want? What is important – is it ourselves? Our own prosperity and security? Or is it *each other*? Should they vote to quell their fears, or vote to champion their hopes? And that's what we're going to show them today – we're going to go out there, and we're going to help them see that hope is stronger than fear. That justice is more powerful than self-interest. That *we don't need to live in a world like this one.*"

The rainbow began to murmur in approval, then cheer, and sporadic clusters of applause broke out as Dave spoke.

"If this town elects the British English Emancipation

Front, something dark and awful will plant a flag in our society. Not only do we have to stop them from winning, but we also have to win a battle that is going on beneath the ballot-box, beneath the surface. We need to win the hearts of the electorate, who in these turbulent times will be forever tempted by people like BEEF and their simplistic, scapegoating solutions. We need to win this seat, and we need to win this debate!"

At that, the rainbow erupted, and Dave could barely be heard over the cheers.

"So, go out there, and fight today not just for a party, or for an election, but for a simple truth – that we are all different, and we are all the same, and that by serving each other we secure our whole world!"

And with Dave's words ringing in their ears and in their hearts, an army of HHHP activists poured out of Green House, and into the febrile atmosphere of a town about to choose between them, and BEEF.

9

"Good morning Sandport, you're listening to Danny Gray on Coastal FM and it's a beautiful Wednesday morning! Today is the final day of the election campaign, and this is Sandport Decides! We're coming to you live from Sandport community hall with this special show in which *you*, the people of Sandport, can ask their parliamentary candidates any question they like!"

"Well, not quite any question, Danny," joked Simon.

"Ha ha, no that's right Simon – we don't want to know about inside leg measurements or whatever! No, this is about the *issues*."

Sandport community hall had not seen this much media exposure since a boy scout jamboree several years ago in which a live python escaped during a skit and attempted to consume Muriel, who ran the refreshments table. After being dislodged by the Scoutmaster with a fire extinguisher, the python slithered out into the night to become a leading theory for Sandport's oddly high rate of cat disappearances.

Four-hundred Sandportian bottoms filled every chair in the hall, and the walls had been decked out in giant Coastal

FM logos and 'Sandport Decides' banners. Danny and Simon stood on a simple black stage, several stools arranged in a semicircle for the candidates. A large screen hung above them, projecting a chart with colourful, snaking lines emanating from the candidates' faces.

The travails of the HHHP and the possibility of the far-right winning its first parliamentary seat had attracted TV news cameras from national and international channels. Outside, a crowd of enthusiastic HHHP supporters cheered as the broadcast began, separated by police officers from a large crowd of BEEF activists – whose cheers were notably several octaves down from the HHHP's and altogether angrier.

Excelsior Thorne, sitting at ease on a stool, was the only candidate that had actually turned up. The Labour candidate had found that her car wouldn't start. The Liberal Democrat had found a mysterious last-minute e-mail informing her of a change of venue. The Conservative candidate had found himself locked on his estate by a malfunctioning security gate. The Green candidate, alarmingly, had not been found at all.

Alicia and Bart stood in the wings.

"He's neck-and-neck with Dave Williams," said Bart, his face glowing above his phone. "Latest poll. This might be the most important debate of the election, and Williams hasn't even turned up."

"There he is," said Alicia, nodding as Dave, Rufus and Dillon appeared in the other wing across the stage. Dave strode out onto the stage, showered, shaved and resplendent in a dark suit and open-necked shirt.

Danny acknowledged Dave as he perched on one of the stools. "Okay," he said. "Let's get started. It seems we have only David Williams of the Happening Happy Hippy Party and Excelsior Thorne of the British English Emancipation Front, but that should make for a great debate."

"It certainly should, Danny!" said Simon. "And remember, everybody in the audience has a handheld voting device so that we can see how candidate responses resonate – or don't – with the audience."

Danny cleared his throat and seemed to turn his enthusiasm dial down a notch or two, presumably to convey gravity. "Let's take our first question. Bill, of Albemarle Street, with a question for Excelsior Thorne."

Somewhere in the audience a chair screeched back a couple of inches, and a small man in a grey shirt stood up. A boom mic reached over him like a robotic giraffe.

"Yeah, um, do you think that crime is out of control in Sandport, and what will you do about it?"

Thorne stood and walked to the centre of the stage. His suit, tie and tie-pin had all been selected to convert his appearance from portly to statesmanly. Alicia watched him run through the mental body language checklist – confident gait, open gestures, calm demeanour. Look like an MP. A really good MP.

"That's a great question, Bill," he said. "I think crime *is* out of control in Sandport. And we all know the solution here, so let's not let political correctness get in the way. We need well-funded police, stronger laws against anti-social behaviour, and better controls on who we let into this country!"

There was a brief smattering of applause, and Danny looked to Dave for his response.

"Wow," said Dave. "There it is again. Dog-whistle politics, trying to blame the marginalised in our society without the courage to spell it out or the evidence to back it up. Bill, Sandport is not in the middle of a crime wave. We have a great society here, people of all walks of life working and living together. Sure, we need to do more about all the issues that any town has– drug rehabilitation, employment, looking again at the opportunities we create for our young people. But we don't do that by picking on any one section of our community. We do it by working together, and last night we saw graffiti and criminal damage with frankly racist intent – and that's the kind of behaviour we need to address."

That generated a slightly louder and more enthusiastic applause from the audience, but it died off as Thorne retorted immediately.

"The Happening Happy Hippy Party talking about law and order," he laughed. "You know, I think you've got a cheek even coming here. On police bail for money-laundering? The subject of a major investigation? We don't want crooks in parliament, Mr Williams, and we don't want you!"

There was a loud roar of approval from much of the audience, and a blast of applause.

Bart smirked. "First blood to Excelsior Thorne."

MARTHA WAS IMPRESSED. The FCU had looked like any other anonymous building on a sterile business park. But inside, and wearing a plastic visitor card on a lanyard, she found herself in a magical theme park of technology and information.

Giant displays relayed feeds from news channels and databases all over the world. Multi-lingual operators chatted into headsets with journalists and researchers on six continents. Private intelligence firms were a phone call away, giving them access to everything from satellite imagery to human sources. If it were possible to find the truth at all these days, the FCU stood a good chance.

Paul had introduced them to Mia, a twenty-something researcher with long, black hair that tumbled over her strappy-topped, extensively-tattooed shoulders. She sat at a workstation covered in keyboards, displays and touch-screens and nodded politely at Martha, the Panther and Catie.

"Mia's been working for most of the night on this," said Paul.

Dutifully, Mia held up a can of energy drink. "Behold, my weapon," she said. She was Canadian. Martha liked the accent.

"Well, we're very grateful, Mia," said Catie. "What do you have?"

Paul nodded. "I'll leave you to it," he said, and spun round.

"Get comfortable," said Mia, taking a slurp of her energy drink and clattering at her keyboard. "And I'll tell you a story. Do you guys like Shakespeare?"

"I love Shakespeare," smiled Martha, and studiously avoided Catie's eye-roll.

"Well, today's story is Romeo and Juliet, African geopo-litical remake. You know, like, Ridley Scott did it or some-thing. So, let's meet Romeo."

Mia jabbed a return key, and a giant display on the wall burst into a collage of news articles. "The government of Kundunga, the small diamond-rich West African country perfect for your next holiday – were it not in the grip of a civil war. And ruled by a kleptocratic oligarchy."

"I know Kundunga well," said the Panther.

Mia shrugged. "Sure. And hey, the local coffee's good and poverty's great for the exchange rate, am I right?

Anyway, Romeo is not the most handsome hero, unless your idea of romance is the brutal suppression of the innocent. Me, I prefer flowers. So, Romeo's got two special friends here, Kenneth Obi and Anthony Uba. These guys are super-rich, with dirty fingers in every stinking pile in West Africa. Journalists vanish, police investigations close down. Now, these guys are especially powerful interests in Kundunga, where they pretty much control the government. In fact, their corruption was a major factor for the anti-government movement that sparked the civil war. Hold that thought."

Mia took another gulp of her drink, and tapped her screen a few more times.

"Okay, now, meet Juliet. This is the website of Stockade Group, a British weapons wholesaler. They've put military hardware in the hands of dozens of dictatorships worldwide. Stockade are the ice-cream van for every spoilt-brat tyrant who wants yummy treats. If you trace the dots, you find that they've been scratching around for British government clearance to supply weapons to Kundunga. That's a big no-no – only the truly idiotic would think that Kundunga wouldn't use those weapons on its own citizens."

"British defence companies are out of control in West Africa," said Martha. "The NCA have just launched a big new investigation into British Defence Enterprises."

Mia nodded, and paused for a moment. "Are you familiar with the term 'drown the fish'?" She asked.

"A fish can be drowned," said the Panther. "You must hold it in place under the water. It will not be able to move the water over its gills, so it will suffocate."

"I'm not," said Catie. "And that sounds pretty brutal."

"Well don't worry, no animals were harmed in the making of this metaphor," said Mia. "Drown the fish is when you want to keep someone out of the way, so you overload them with work."

"Loading up the NCA's corruption unit with big jobs like BDE would help to prevent it pulling the threads on anything it heard about Stockade," said Martha.

"Exactly. So, there's our star-crossed lovers, but darn it – there are those pesky permits in the way. So hard these days to sell guns! All that paperwork. Romeo and Juliet need Friar Laurence, someone who can bring them together."

Mia's fingers skittered across a touchscreen, and the giant display burst into a spidery diagram of interlinked faces, pictures and captions.

"Meet Ryan Callaghan," she said. "Ryan's an executive at Wishbone, a consultancy that helps to arrange deals between arms companies and African governments."

"That's amazing," said Martha. "How do you know that?"

Mia shrugged. "LinkedIn."

"Yes," said the Panther. "That is Mr Ryan Callaghan. That is his face."

"THE NEXT QUESTION is from Susan, of Bak –"

Danny Gray couldn't even finish his introduction as Susan's voice began squawking from the audience.

"My boy can't afford to go to university because of the fees! But I see all these foreign students coming in. What would you do about that?"

Danny nodded. "Okay, that one to David Williams."

"Susan," said Dave. "We can't be the country we want to be if student tuition fees are a barrier. We would abolish them and return to a grant system. We need to invest in the next generation of minds, now more than ever."

Susan's head bobbed in grumpy agreement, but there was a spike in her question – and Thorne was not slow in seizing it.

"Typical politician dodge, there," he said. "You know, the education system in this country is broken. Crazy courses with no value – madness. And you know what else is madness? The way we prioritise foreign kids over our own!"

"You've got no basis for that allegation, Excelsior," said Dave. "Foreign students are an important part of our economy and our society, and they pay –"

"We're about putting Britain first again, that's all," interrupted Thorne. "And that should be the duty of any British government – to put its own people first."

"Well, it's a funny old thing," said Dave. "When people say things like that, they usually mean only certain types of Briton to be put first. Usually the white middle-class or economic elite. What would you do about tuition fees? You wouldn't get rid of them, would you?"

Above their heads, the black line of BEEF and the orange line of the HHHP danced together, weaving across each other.

"Why are you even here?" asked Thorne, with a theatrical shrug. "Shouldn't you resign, David? Do you disrespect the electorate, and hold your party in such contempt, that you will cling to power *no matter what*?"

At that, the orange line began to dip below the black one.

MARTHA STOOD at the giant display, her face bathed in its glow, lips pursed and arms folded. "This is – very impressive. So, what do you think is going on here, Mia?"

Mia sat back and put her sneakers up on her desk. "I think that the Kundungan government wants weapons, and Stockade wants to provide them. Obi and Uba want to keep the government they control in place. So, Wishbone gets hired to do the dirty work – which in this case is shepherding a massive bribe from Obi and Uba to the British government to grant the clearances. But the money doesn't go into an official's pocket, it goes to this guy Mortimer – apparently via a chain of transfers that includes a bank account set up in Kundunga in Dave Williams' name – and then on to you."

"And what about Mortimer, Mia?" asked Catie.

"There are some pieces of identity data floating about for Mortimer, but nothing that can be verified, and nothing that couldn't have been invented. So, it's entirely possible that the guy's fictitious. But that's not even the most interesting thing."

"What is the most interesting thing?" asked the Panther.

"Small businesses are being strangled by big supermarkets and online shopping. What will you do to protect the high street life of our town?"

"And that's from Helen Gent, who owns an independent pharmacy," said Danny. "Mr Thorne, to you first."

Thorne nodded. "Hey Helen, look, I'm a businessman. And I'm a really successful one. I've had a lot of companies, and I'm super-rich. So, I know how it works. I can negotiate, I'll protect you. You know, protection is what we're about. Standing up for your interests. Who better to protect you from big business, than a big businessman?"

"Helen, Mr Thorne is exactly the kind of 'businessman'

who is destroying the independent businesses of our town," said Dave. "It would be like making a shark the lifeguard at a swimming pool."

"That's an extraordinary allegation," snapped Thorne.

"Is it, though, Mr Thorne? Helen, look him up online – you'll see what Thorne stands for. You'll need to – because his answer didn't tell you a jot about what he'll do for you. Let me tell you what we stand for. We think small, local businesses are more sustainable and better for Britain than big, faceless corporations. We want diverse, independent high streets and exciting local communities. So, if you look at our manifesto, you'll see loads of proposals to increase local investment, capacity-build local businesspeople, promote credit unions and skills exchanges."

"Here's what I'm hearing," said Thorne. "I'm hearing 'yada-yada-yada-politico-speak'. 'Increase local investment'? What does that even mean?"

"It means –"

"There's a crisis on the high street *now*, Mr Williams!" said Thorne. "Right now! We need urgent, forceful action, and we need protection! And all you've got is talk – which is pretty rich, given that you've never owned a business, run a business, heck – you've not even been employed your entire life! And you're up here, talking about 'skills exchanges'? You, David Williams, are a liability to your own party – never mind Sandport!"

"Resign, Williams!" shouted a voice from the audience.

The orange line juddered further beneath the slowly climbing black one.

"This isn't going well," murmured Dillon, slipping out his phone.

"THE MOST INTERESTING THING, is these guys," said Mia, tapping her touchscreen and filling the display with photographs. "Wishbone is owned and operated by a few city businessmen with serious connections. They were at a private Berkshire boys' school with the Prime Minister – in the same school year, actually, and you can see them in photos with him as recently as January. They're also donors to his party."

Martha nodded. "So, you've got the PM at Mortimer's grave, linked to the company handling the money, and heading up the government that gives the clearances that the money is apparently paying for."

"More than that," said Mia. "Whoever set up the deal in Africa had to have the intention that the money was going to go to the HHHP, or they wouldn't have *created the Williams account in Kundunga*."

"There's a fifth connection too," said Catie, grimly. "Amy Cordell. One of the PM's spin doctors, appears mysteriously at HHHP Central, 'wanting to help', at the same time the money is paid. And then vanishes just as Dave and Rufus get arrested."

"But I don't see why," said Martha. "I get it – but I'm not seeing the motive. Why would the PM want the HHHP to have enough money to fight a national campaign?"

"A distraction?" shrugged Catie. "And more importantly – is this enough evidence?"

"It's a lot of good stuff," said Martha, glancing at Mia. "But it needs human sources."

"I can be your human source," said the Panther. "I will tell the world of this corruption!"

"But you'll be prosecuted," said Catie. "Or worse. Won't Uba and Obi come after you?"

"Of course. But I will disappear. I always disappear. That is why they call me the Panther. I have the stealth."

"That is very noble of you," said Martha. "And that covers the origin of the money, but you still can't bring in the PM strongly enough."

"I can keep looking," said Mia, handing Martha a flash drive. "Here's everything we've got for now."

Catie's phone rang, and she raised it to her ear. "Hi, Dillon, what's up? Oh really? Okay – okay we'll be right over."

"Trouble at mill?" asked Martha.

Catie jammed her phone in her pocket. "Dave's tanking at Sandport Decides. Thorne's hammering the arrest with every question. Mia, thank you – we need to get to the community hall now."

ON THE HUGE screen above Dave and Thorne, the orange line now shuffled along considerably below the black one.

"Okay," said Danny. "Our last question is from, er, Peter Trousers – a local businessman. This question to David Williams, first."

"It's pronounced *Tru-serge*, actually," said Peter, from near the front. "Mr Williams, we have watched your party go from being a couple of stoners who hung out in an old public toilet to a political machine in the space of a few months. How can we be sure that if we elect you, you won't transform just as easily into just the kind of MP that you're standing against?"

Dave couldn't see the display above his head, and he couldn't hear the whispered desperation of Dillon and Rufus in the wings. But he could see Thorne inflating like a cobra, inhaling the scale and enthusiasm of the applause shifting towards him. Thorne wasn't even using the arrest like an escape button, a way to deflect difficult questions. He was using it like a return key, punctuating every paragraph with it. And the audience loved it.

"Come on, Dave!" shouted a lone, encouraging voice from the audience.

Dave searched his mind for something to say, but nothing came. And as the uncomfortable silence became exponentially more uncomfortable, a conversation with Catie popped into his head. *Apparently questions don't have answers. They have 'replies'*, said his voice. *Sure,* said Catie. *Sometimes they do, though.*

With nothing ready to come out, Dave opened his mouth. To answer the question.

"You can't," he said, with a shrug. "You can't be sure, Peter. You can't be sure that any candidate won't turn into the thing you elected them to oppose. And I won't pretend that we've had to shape up in order to try to represent you. But we've told you what we believe, and what we plan to do. What Sandport needs to worry about isn't the HHHP failing to keep their promises. It's BEEF *keeping* theirs."

With that, there was a loud cheer, and a renewed blast of applause. The orange line edged up a little.

"Another dodge," boomed Thorne as the applause subsided. "Another half-answer. He agreed with your fears, actually, Peter – David Williams can't guarantee that the HHHP's ascent to the establishment won't stop here. But with BEEF, you can see our track record behind us. We've been fighting for your rights, fighting for Britain, for decades!"

"Fighting against *whom*, Thorne?" Stormed Dave, angrily. "Who *isn't* Britain, to you?"

"Well!" said Danny. "I think we've –"

"No!" shouted Dave, silencing Danny with his palm and crossing the floor to draw himself up to Thorne. "This is the most important moment of this entire debate!"

"Bloody hell," said Dillon, as the hall fell into the most noiseless silence it had ever known.

"Who *isn't* British, Thorne?" demanded Dave. "Who doesn't qualify to be in your Britain?"

Thorne, who had been visibly stunned by Dave's passion, started to rally. "Now, David, I –"

"Is it Muslims, Thorne?" asked Dave. "Is it Sikhs? Jewish people? The LGBTI community? Anyone who migrated? Anyone whose parents migrated? Anyone whose grandparents migrated? Anyone with a skin tone darker than magnolia? Anyone with an accent? Is it those receiving benefits? Is it the mentally ill? Is it anyone else who has been marginalised, or mocked, or targeted by your supporters? Exactly who is left, Thorne? Who is left?"

Thorne's cheeks were reddening now, and Dave could see the vein in the centre of his head throbbing. But he didn't care. He didn't care at all.

"You don't get to choose who counts as British, and you don't get to dominate the minorities. Because sooner or later, you dominate so many different minorities that they become the majority, and the spell is broken. Tomorrow, Sandport is going to make sure that spell *never gets cast*."

Thorne glanced up at the giant display, and shrugged. "Is it?"

MARTHA, at the wheel of her Mini, blinked as Danny Gray's

voice, oddly comforting given the circumstances, filled the airwaves.

"Well that's the end of our questions, and I want to thank both Mr Thorne and Mr Williams for a really great debate."

"Oh yeah, one for the pages of history," added Simon's voice.

"There's just time to check the polling – and yes, it looks like BEEF have come out on top. Mr Thorne, you've won today's debate!"

There was a cheer from the audience, and applause, and Martha switched off the radio.

"Wow," she said. "So, your guy went for it a bit, there."

Catie tapped her hand against the armrest as the mini arrived at the community hall. The road was blocked by police cars, two cordons of officers separating BEEF and HHHP supporters. BEEF's were louder, and more aggressive, but the HHHP's made up the difference in the volume, diversity and colour of their placards. TV crews looked on, the tension in the air captured in the national memory forever. Martha waved her press card to a constable that peered through the windscreen, and he opened a barrier to let them into the hall's car park.

"This is what they wanted," said Catie, as Martha drove past broadcast vans and trailers.

"What?"

"Division. The government wanted division. That's why they wanted us to run a national campaign – so that we would split the opposition vote. And then, they wanted us destroyed close to the election, so that there would be disillusion and a low turnout. That's why Amy came, that's why she helped us to do so well. She was working for them."

"If that is what they have done, then it is a very risky

strategy," said the Panther, as Martha parked up next to a clutch of smoking stagehands. "The forces of populism are powerful and unwieldy. You must be wary that what you unleash cannot always be controlled. As we say in Kundunga – if you try to cage the river, be careful that you do not drown."

They opened the doors and stepped out into the crisp morning.

"You're probably right," said Martha. "But we can't prove it. And until you can, all the FCU has done is make it worse for the HHHP. Now it's not just the pretty opaque 'money-laundering', now it's corrupt arm deals and goodness knows what else."

They walked across the car park just as Dillon, Rufus and Dave emerged from a back entrance. Dillon was frowning – something Catie hadn't seen before. Rufus was looking at the floor as he walked. Dave looked shaken.

"We're out of time, aren't we?" said Catie. It was a statement, not a question.

"Dillon, what happened?" asked Martha, as the two groups converged.

Dillon sighed. "Thorne hammered Dave on the arrests. It was his go-to for every debate point, and the crowd lapped it up. We started two points down on their voting thing and finished twenty down."

"Damn it," said Catie. "We shouldn't have put him on."

"No, we should," said Dillon, nodding. "We had to try. But we really need this *Chronicle* piece. Did we get what we needed at the FCU? Are we – cleared?"

"I'm sorry," said Catie, shaking her head. "Not quite. There's a lot – we know where the money probably came from, but we can't prove the motive. And we can't rope the Prime Minister in tightly enough."

Dillon bit his lip. "Then we're in trouble. We're in serious trouble."

"No, this is great!" said Rufus. Catie and Dillon looked at him.

"How?" asked Dillon. "How on earth is it great to be this far behind, the night before the election?"

"It's our *Empire Strikes Back* moment! You know, everything looks glum and someone's had his hand cut off. Excelsior Thorne is Dave's dad, that sort of thing. But it means that *Return of the Jedi* is just around the corner – a big, happy victory with dancing teddy bears!"

Dillon looked away. "Wait – Dave?"

Dave had approached the stagehands and obtained a cigarette, which he was lighting up.

"Wow," said Dillon. "I haven't seen that in a long time."

"Is he okay?" asked Catie.

"He had kind of a meltdown. Did you hear?"

"We heard," said Martha. "I thought it might work. It hit your differentiators – passion, authenticity, honesty."

Loud, patriotic classical music filled the car park, and they looked up to see the BEEF Mercedes arriving as Thorne and his team walked out of the hall. Thorne smiled and waved.

"Fun morning, hippies, thanks for a good time," he said, and then glanced over to Dave, the smile dropping away. "Don't smoke too many of those, Williams," he said. "They'll destroy you."

Thorne smirked, and ducked into the car. The crowds outside roared in a queasy combination of delight and fury as the Mercedes passed through the police cordon.

The Happening Happy Hippy Party stood in silence for a moment.

"What do we do, now?" asked Rufus.

DAVE THANKED the gentleman that had donated a cigarette, and disposed of it. He rubbed his eyes, and began to walk back over to party leaders huddled next to Martha's Mini.

He felt oddly at peace, reflecting that maybe he wouldn't change a thing about this experience. They may be facing defeat, but contrary to popular belief, a victory at the ballot box was not the only victory. What they had learned, their renewed love for each other, even the briefest glimpse of something wonderful with Amy – none of these things were defeats. They were all steps to victory. Shorter steps than they had hoped, perhaps – but steps nonetheless.

The others quietened as he arrived, and looked up at him. He let his eyes drift across their faces.

"What do we do, now?" repeated Rufus.

Dave turned to Martha. "What are you going to write?"

Martha glanced at Catie. "Just what I have, I guess," she said. "That was the deal. Your money probably came from an arms deal in a war-torn African country."

"Well," he sighed. "At least it'll make our Wikipedia page more interesting. Come on, let's get in the bus and go back to Green House. What will be, will be."

Dillon nodded. "We did our best."

Dave was about to reply, and then he heard another voice he recognised.

"Dave," it called out.

He turned around, as did the others – and there was Amy Cordell, standing at the police cordon.

"Amy," he called out. "That's Amy!"

"Wow," said Dillon.

Rufus ran over to the cordon and whispered something

to a police officer, who ushered her through. She marched rapidly up to Dave and, before he could ask anything, said:

"I've betrayed you."

For Dave, everything seemed to stop for a moment – his mind a puddle of stillness as the political storm swirled around them. He had so many questions, and in this moment, none of them came. None of them at all.

"I – I don't understand," he said. "You left."

Catie touched his arm. "Dave, come on, let's get on the bus. Amy, you're not welcome here, please go away."

"Amy, what happened?" asked Dave. "Where did you go? Why?"

Amy took a step closer, and for a moment Dave thought she was going to reach for his hand, but she didn't.

"Just – Dave, listen. Listen to me. It was a plot. The money, Winstanley Mortimer, me. Downing Street tried to use the HHHP to save the government."

Catie glanced at Martha, her face triumphant. "I knew it!"

"I don't understand," said Dave. "I don't understand why the PM was interested in us. I don't understand any of this."

"Come on," said Catie, without looking at Amy. "Let's go."

"Sure, but – just a moment, Catie," said Dave. "Amy, what do you mean, you betrayed us – what is the plot? What's happening?"

Amy cleared her throat. "The PM wanted to make sure you became a success. So, he sent me here to help you. He wanted to split the ballot box and create apathy, so that there would be a low turnout and opposition votes would be spread between the other parties."

"And he would be re-elected," said Dave.

Amy nodded. "I'm so sorry. I – I was different, then. I was a different person. Then I met you, then I realised who you guys are and what you believe. And I changed, I swear. You changed me. That's why I left. Because I couldn't lie to you anymore."

"Can you prove this, Amy?" asked Martha.

"I was there," she said.

Martha and Catie exchanged glances.

"Will you go on the record?" asked Martha.

"It'll end your political career," said Catie, evenly.

"Not if you stay with us," said Dave. "You'll always have a job with us."

Amy stared at him. "Are you kidding? After *this*? How can you trust me, after this?"

Dave shrugged. "We believe in second chances. Let's take a vote – readmitting Amy into the party."

Dave looked around. Rufus nodded with enthusiasm. Dillon also gave a nod.

Catie was looking at Amy.

"I bloody knew it, Amy," she said. "What did I say to you, back in that hotel? And more to the point, what did you say to me?"

"Catie – " began Dave, but Amy waved him back.

"I said I'd earn your trust," Amy admitted.

Catie shrugged. "I didn't want to be right about you, Amy."

Amy nodded. "I'm not asking to be forgiven. Just for the chance to make this right."

"Well," she sighed. "It's taken great strength of character to come back, Amy. And even more to sacrifice your career to put things right." Catie nodded to Dave. "Okay."

"See!" said Rufus. "Teddy bears!"

"Okay," said Martha. "I'll call Jock and we'll get this in

tonight's edition. Amy, you ride back with me and we'll talk."

Dave turned back to Amy, his face close to hers. "Are you sure you want to do this?"

"More than anything," she said. "Integrity, authenticity, hope – remember?"

"Could you even – be arrested?"

"I'll take that risk," she said.

"I don't know if it will be enough in time to change what happens tomorrow," said Dillon.

"Don't be too sure," replied Amy. "This debate was important but it wasn't everything. Get this story out tonight, make sure it floods the airwaves – and you've had a doorstep campaign out today, right?"

"Yes – Riz and Harry have been running it."

"There you go. Never underestimate the simple power of real people having real conversations. And don't forget your unpredictable age and demographic profile. You might be surprised."

"I hate to rush you guys," said Martha. "We need to get moving on this, now."

A FEW HOURS LATER, Martha sat at her computer in Big Sue's vegan café, her phone to her ear and listening to a dial tone. It was odd, she thought – she always assumed that the most important moments in political history were accompanied by a sense of gravity. That somehow there would be dramatic music, and cold visual filters. But, in fact, there was just the solid wall of *normal* – her, sitting in a café, next to a half a cup of cold soy latte and a frankly inedible muffin.

"Hello!" said Jock's voice, above a continuous, high-pitched roar.

"Jock, hi, it's Martha."

"Arthur? Who's Arthur?"

"It's quite a bad line, Jock – what are you doing? It's *Martha*."

"Oh, Martha, hi! Martha I'm playing a drinking game with some lovely models I met at a fashion show! Tiffany is only twenty-one, you know!"

"Jock, it's lunchtime –"

"That's a good point, Martha! Jo-Jo, I'm putting you in charge of getting us some food when we land!"

"Land? Are you – are you in plane?"

"Not at all!" boomed Jock's voice. "We're in my helicopter! You should try it, every time you see a landmark you recognise you have to drop a shot of that cinnamon schnapps stuff with gold bits floating about in it!"

"Jock," said Martha. "Jock you're not flying it, are you?"

"No!"

"Thank goodness."

"We're taking it in turns! It's hard to hold onto the stick-thing and slam a shot at the same time! I've got Scarlett on my lap, working the pedals! She's twenty, you know! What's that? Oh, sorry, *nineteen*!"

"Jock I'm going to get off the line because this sounds very dangerous, and you need to concentrate," said Martha, as girlish voices whooped in the background. "I just need you to clear a front-page story for this evening. It's a world-exclusive, and it's dynamite."

"We're not running the thing about the hygiene of the toilets on the ferry anymore? Lily you've fallen out of your bikini there, you cheeky girl! Whoops!"

"No – this is about the PM, who took a bribe from an

African arms deal and used it to interfere with the election. I have two sources, and a load of research."

"Big Ben! Drink!" shouted Jock. "Hang on, we'll do it again as we come round! Yeah, Martha, that sounds fine. Bye now!"

"Thanks, Jock," said Martha.

"Sorry, my lovelies," Jock was saying as she hung up. "One of the lasses at work wants to put something new on the front page, sounds like a heart-warming story about someone in a tribe in Afghanistan who's a queer electrician."

THE *SANDPORT CHRONICLE*'S most successful story of all time had the headline 'Ice cream man retires: Town in shock'. Its second most successful story was 'Parish centre fish pond controversy'. But the community-shattering revelations of ice cream vendors and minor landscaping were eclipsed that Wednesday evening, when the front page carried 'Corruption, murder, arms deals: Prime Minister in shock allegations.'

The *Chronicle* had never sold out before, but within hours there were no more copies anywhere in Sandport. But that didn't matter, because the story was all over the world in time for the evening news. The Prime Minister's face – and a picture of Dave at his most innocent – were emblazoned across every major television news channel, their names sprawled over the radio waves, and the internet ablaze with memes.

It had also, of course, made its way to Downing Street.

"What the hell is this?" stormed the Prime Minister, throwing the newspaper at Starling. The *Sandport Chronicle* had not been designed with air travel in mind, and it fluttered unhelpfully to the floor beneath him.

"It's the chickens coming home to roost, sir," said Starling, rubbing his eyes. "I told you this was a bad idea."

"Who publishes this tosh? This is one of Jock Mason's rags, isn't it? I'll have his balls ripped off and thrown to the pigeons for this. Stephanie!"

The door opened and one of the Prime Minister's aides appeared.

"Yes sir?"

"Get me Jock Mason on the phone!"

"Yes sir," she said, and scurried out again.

"And you!" said the Prime Minister, pointing at Starling. "You! What do you have to say about this, newspaper-wrangler-in-chief-up-my-arse?"

"Me?" said Starling, raising his voice to the Prime Minister for the first time in their relationship. "*Me*? I've done everything I could to stop Fleet Street from sniffing up the trouser-leg on this one! Everything! I've worked, and worked, and worked! I've had about two hours sleep a night this campaign, the same amount of sleep I've been getting ever since I started working for you! My wife's moved out, my angina's roaring, and there's only so much I can do to keep you up in the polls and out of trouble if you're going to be hatching crazy schemes!"

The Prime Minister was silent for a moment. When he spoke, it was low, and dark.

"You're going to contain this," he said, placing his forefinger on Starling's chest. "You're going to make this go away. This libel, this half-baked conspiracy theory. Or *you're* going to go away, Starling."

"Libel? It's true! Every bloody word of it is true!"

"No it isn't – it's lies, all lies, and we're going to tell everybody it's lies! You're going to go out there and tell everybody that this is screaming, hysterical, unhinged guano and –"

"The truth?"

The Prime Minister's eyes widened.

"Truth?" he shouted. "What is 'truth'?"

There was a knock at the door, and the Prime Minister's assistant appeared again, this time accompanied by two moustachioed men in suits and raincoats. The suits looked cheap to Starling – off the rack and ill-fitting.

"Sir," she said. "This is Detective Chief Inspector Rydell, and Detective Sergeant Pike, both from the Metropolitan Police."

"Good!" snarled the Prime Minister, pointing to the pile of crumpled newspaper on the floor. "About time someone took this libel seriously. What are you going to do about all this, then?"

Rydell cleared his throat. "Prime Minister," he said. "You do not have to say anything, but it may harm your defence if you fail to mention, when questioned, anything you later rely on in court. Anything you do say may be taken down in evidence."

10

The Prime Minister had resigned by midnight, leaving his party fighting a desperate, doomed campaign of damage limitation. And true to her word, Amy visited Sandport police station in the early hours of the morning to explain what she knew.

As the media storm roared, Dave had managed to catch an hour or two's sleep. He had wanted to help Amy and Catie plan the party response, but had been persuaded that he would be most useful if he were a bit more rested – not so tired that kept forgetting how to spell 'Sandport'.

And then, as the sun rose and Britain woke up, the parade of radio and television interviews started. Dave found himself on sofas, in front of green-screens and behind microphones in studios all over London.

The angle of Martha's piece was the HHHP's efforts to clear its name. As they read it in the paper, both Amy and Catie agreed that they could treat the matter as a human interest story, enabling the HHHP to reach a wider group of voters, with a raw honesty that enhanced Dave's credibility.

And so, while the other parties demanded inquiries, and

catcalled and fumed into the television cameras, Dave smiled and talked about their determination in the face of adversity, their commitment to the truth and being guided by hope, not fear. It was feel-good television, and it sent Britain to the ballot boxes feeling good about the Happening Happy Hippy Party.

Outside Green House, police officers held back crowds of reporters and admirers as Dave and Riz stepped out of their car, relieved to be home after their hectic morning in the capital, and hurried into the relative calm of the lobby.

It dawned on Dave that the majority of things said to him that morning had a question mark on the end. And as he walked onto the busy main office floor, alive with the hum of activity and the birdcall of a dozen ringing phones, it was clear that the questions had not stopped. Catie and her team were fielding call after call from journalist after journalist, holding the press at bay while Amy directed the rest of the HHHP in a colossal 'get out the vote' campaign.

He found most of the party leadership in Catie's office, and she smiled at him as he arrived, speaking hurriedly into her phone.

"Well I disagree with that," she was saying. "We are really optimistic about what's going to happen in Sandport today."

Catie covered the handset with her hand. "Welcome back," she said. "Get yourself a coffee and then Amy wants you on the phone bank."

"I think if I have any more caffeine I could probably just sprint from house to house, never mind call them. How, er, are things with –?"

Catie smiled. "Fine," she said, and turned back to her phone. "No, Sandport is *definitely* a swing constituency. It couldn't be more swing if it was picking car keys out of a fruit-bowl with five other constituencies. Okay, thanks, bye now."

Dave looked out at the open-plan office. The phone bank was in full flow, operators chatting away at some of the only computer terminals left after the police raid. White-boards displayed the morning's fresh talking-points. He could hear people laughing. He could see the smiles. There was a warm atmosphere, a sense of relief and energy. A confidence, almost.

"Hi Dave," said Dillon, who was peering out of the window into the street. "How was London?"

"London, to me, is increasingly a place where I go to be argued with or interrogated," replied Dave, taking off his coat. "What's outside?"

"Sandport seems oddly full of campervans today," he murmured.

"I should hope so," replied Catie, returning to her laptop. "The South Coast Volkswagen Campervan Club are helping us to give voters free lifts of the polling stations. Amy set it up."

Rufus appeared at the door, his hand over his phone. "I've got a journo here clarifying our position on the war in the Middle East. Would we pull Britain out?"

"We're against war in general," replied Catie.

"Generale? Where's that? Who are they at war with?"

"No, Rufus – I mean, we generally oppose war."

"Oh, I see. So, whether it's the fighting in Generale or anywhere else, we're against it?"

"Rufus, there is no fighting in Generale! Generale is not a place!"

"Got it," said Rufus, turning back to his call and walking out. "Yeah, so, because it's not a real place, we would pull Britain out of that war, yes."

Dave looked up, alarmed, but Catie waved him off. "Rufus could go for one of his special naked jogs through parliament and it wouldn't make the news this morning. Don't worry."

The next person to appear in Catie's doorway was Amy, holding a notebook and with a phone earpiece just visible beneath her hair.

"Welcome back to base camp," she smiled. "Come on, chores to do."

Amy led Dave to the phone bank, sat him down in front a screen and offered him a headset.

"Click on that button, then that button, and then be as charming as you can to the human voice you hear on the other end of the line," she instructed, pointing at each in turn.

"Charming," he repeated, glancing at the screen and grabbing the mouse. "I can do charming."

Dave sat back as the phone rang. "So, Amy," he said. "I was wondering, tomorrow night, when all this is over, if you wanted to maybe get some dinner?"

She smiled and perched on the desk. "I always like dinner."

"I mean, I'd be there too, right – that's the arrangement I'm offering. Dinner with me."

"I got that, No-bama."

"You know, I was thinking we could try out some different politically-themed nicknames. I was thinking, maybe, Chairman Wow?"

Amy cocked her head to one side. "Feeble Castro?"

"Okay, well, perhaps we can negotiate," Dave replied, turning back to his handset. "Hi! I'm David Williams from the HHHP and I'm calling to ask if you need help to get to a polling station today?"

ALICIA RHODES CLOSED her front door and set off for her polling station, the morning frost twinkling in the election day sunlight. It was cold, but quiet – a moment of peace to savour after the chaos of the night. Her feet crunched down the driveway to her block of flats, a huge Victorian conversion, and with a creak of the gate she strode out into Sandport.

She was unsurprised by the night's developments, and BEEF had drawn even more hope from them. The opportunity was clear; not only were the HHHP all tangled up in something very unattractive, but also now so was the governing party. Thorne had been rolled out to do as many television and radio interviews as possible. Bart had insisted that they should push the advantage. She had agreed.

Alicia turned the corner onto Sandport high street, a sadder place than she remembered it. She walked past the building that had once been a record shop in which she had fawned over the LPs, then cassettes, then CDs of one boyband after another. It had been a pound shop for fifteen years, now. And the aromas of fresh meat, fruit and baking bread were all gone too – the independent butchers, grocers and bakers all replaced by charity shops, discount retailers and huge, national chains.

She turned again, to walk down the road towards the polling station, and she was still lost in her thoughts when everything changed.

The next few seconds happened so quickly that they were over before Alicia realised they had begun. She felt a hard shove from behind, and then a sense that something was missing – her handbag, perhaps? As quickly as that arose, there was an explosion of pain in her forehead and suddenly she was lying on the pavement.

Alicia looked around in dizzy, disconnected confusion. There was a pair of trainers, attached to a pair of jeans, running at speed away from her.

"Stop, thief!" shouted someone, and then a shalwar kameez jumped over her and sprinted after the trainers.

For a moment, Alicia's world spun, and all she knew was the cold wetness of the pavement, the throbbing of her forehead, and the disorientated indignity of staring up at the street from the gutter.

And then, there was a warm, female voice.

"Are you okay? You hit your head on the lamppost. Here, let me help you," it said, and Alicia felt hands on her arms and the comforting scent of perfume.

"What happened?" said Alicia, as the lady helped her to sit up.

"I think you've just been robbed," said the voice. "Do you feel dizzy?"

"I don't know, but thank you," said Alicia, turning around to find that the voice belonged to an Asian woman in her mid-thirties, wearing an attractive cerulean hijab.

Alicia froze. And the woman must have caught the look on Alicia's face, because her smile hardened a little.

"Worried you'll catch the Islam, right?" she said. "Don't worry, it doesn't spread on contact."

Alicia coughed as she used the lamppost to help herself to stand up.

"No, I – I didn't, well. Thank you."

"I'm Aysha," she said.

"Alicia."

The man in the shalwar kameez was jogging back now, visibly empty-handed. He seemed about the same age as

Aysha, handsome, with a well-kept beard and a fashionable jacket.

"Are you okay?" he said. "I'm sorry – I didn't get him, he ran down an alley and I didn't get there in time to see where he went."

"That's okay," said Alicia as she straightened her coat. "Thank you."

The man was looking back up the street. "It was some punk kid. Probably known to the police, I expect. Don't worry, I'll give a witness statement. I have a good description of him. We need to sort these people out."

"This is my husband, Imran," smiled Aysha.

"Hi," nodded Imran. "Pleased to meet you. Sorry about the circumstances."

"Imran," Alicia repeated. "Where are you from, then?"

Imran glanced at Aysha. "Norwich," he shrugged.

"Anyway," said Aysha, hurriedly. "You look like you could do with a nice hot cup of tea and some cake. Come on, let's go – our shout. You can phone the police from the café. And they'll have some ice for your forehead. And maybe we need to get you to the hospital? Just because of your head?"

THE FLIGHT ATTENDANT made his way steadily down the aisle of the economy class cabin, offering plastic cups of water and juice. As the Boeing 747 banked gently, a booming, joyful voice rose above the crying children and snoring.

"Yes, Amadu, I am speaking from the aeroplane! It is true! No, I am in the economy class cabin. Yes, really! Because, Amadu, I have embraced a new philosophy, that is why I am calling. I would like you to collect me from the airport, so that I can share with you the happening happy hippy ideology. I would like you to help me to set up a new political party in Kundunga!"

The flight attendant smiled to the gentleman in 47E, and passed him a cup of water. The Panther smiled back.

ALICIA WAITED as the election officer ran his pencil down a column of names. Her polling station was at a local infant school, the walls bearing the childrens' colourful pictures of what were presumably animals, their families and friends – not terrifying, multi-limbed mutants as they in fact appeared to be.

"Ah, there you are," said the officer, marking her name and handing her a voting card. "Now," he added, nodding to the bruise on her forehead. "Are you sure you're okay, madam?"

Alicia nodded, thanked him, and crossed over to a voting booth. She placed the card down, picked up a pencil, and let it hover over the box next to Excelsior Thorne's name.

She paused.

Alicia had been with BEEF for a very long time. Since it began, in fact – but even then, she had been involved with a number of its predecessor organisations years before that. In fact, since graduating from university, she didn't think she had ever voted for a mainstream political party.

Issues of race, foreigners and pedigree had always marbled through BEEF and its predecessors like thick lines of fat. BEEF's confidence about this had varied over the years; party leaders oscillated between 'I'm not racist, but' and 'well if that's what racism is, call me a racist.' In fact, BEEF had self-defined as a broad church of opinion, and that allowed almost every member – including Alicia – to consider themselves a moderate. There were always people to the left and the right of you. People any further to the left were soft. People any further to the right were dangerous. But that was okay, because you could control them. You were one of the moderates.

The party's public line on these issues had remained relatively consistent. Inside, though, there were fashions. Sometimes the group that drew its focus were Sikhs, sometimes Jews, sometimes black people. One group, of course, had been the main beneficiaries of BEEF's gaze for more than fifteen years now.

But it was neither race nor immigration that had first drawn Alicia to one of BEEF's predecessors all those years ago. It was their social agenda. A younger Alicia had worried that the social rules and values – the 'family' values – by which she had governed her life were being destroyed, with nothing she could trust put in their stead.

Then Britain seemed to start changing. As it did so, she saw people that she didn't know and didn't understand suddenly *here*. And they were here in huge numbers, failing to do her the courtesy of speaking her language, dressing properly and looking after their misbehaving children in public. And to whom were they loyal? How could she trust people who might have different priorities? Where was her Britain?

And then, as the millennium turned, this sense was complemented by a slowly mounting fear that Britain was being taken for a ride. That it wasn't competitive. That mainstream politicians were asleep at the wheel while other countries were taking advantage of Britain through the UN, through foreign aid, through deals badly-negotiated by liberals too weak to defend the country against these powerful cabals.

And then Islam, the great threat – and the great galvanising force for BEEF. Now there was a seemingly monolithic nemesis, one that could transform BEEF from the disassociated fringe into the vanguard, the flawed heroes.

The pieces fell readily into place. It had never been easier to write a manifesto. Things that would have disqualified them from public debate in the nineties were now openly discussed on political television shows. 'Racist' and 'xenophobic' had now become 'edgy' and 'populist'. Was taxing companies for employing foreign workers 'extremist'? Only if most people agreed that it would be extremist. Otherwise it was merely 'controversial'.

And now that BEEF might actually win, she thought – was their manifesto really what she wanted? In the cold light of a Thursday morning, away from the noise and the emotion and the drama, did she really want all that? Would it *really* do good?

Alicia thought of all the mansplaining and gaslighting. She thought of the anger, and the fear, with which the streets seemed to throb – and Thorne's indifference to it as much as Bart's enthusiasm. She thought of the violence, and Thorne's refusal to disassociate from the violent European fascist. She thought of Aysha and Imran. She thought of the future.

Alicia Rhodes made her mark on her voting card.

Eleven forty-five, election night.

All roads lead here, thought Dave as he arrived at the

community hall for a second day running. Zero hour. The polls had closed at ten, the count was nearly complete, and whatever happened next was decided. It was the end of the voyage, and which fresh journey began depended entirely on the people of Sandport.

Amy sat in the back of the car next to him, Riz in the front passenger seat and a staff driver behind the wheel.

"Got both speeches?" she asked.

Dave nodded. "Left jacket pocket for victory, right for defeat."

"Seems apt," shrugged Amy, with a faint smile.

Camera flashes flickered outside while supporters cheered and police officers held back booing BEEF activists. Riz had arranged an electric sedan, and it purred through the gate into the car park, away from the raging fire of people and emotion.

"Let's pull up here, by the back door," said Riz, and the staffer nodded.

Amy leaned over as the car stopped. "Let me check your rosette," she said, her face close enough for Dave to feel its warmth. "Okay. You're good."

They climbed out of the car, breath steaming in the chilly night air, and the rest of the HHHP leadership emerged from a second electric sedan behind them. Wordlessly, they made their way past the security guards and into the community hall.

Inside, the count was in its final moments. Counting officers, fuelled almost entirely by caffeine and sugar, sat at long tables and between piles of paper. Representatives of the competing parties, distinguished by their rosettes, drifted across the sea of silent, concentrated industriousness. After all the money, all the rhetoric, all the drama, British democracy distilled into unpaid volunteers popping jelly babies and placing slips into one pile or another.

He smiled. Good.

"I'll find out how much longer there is until the declaration," said Amy, and walked away to find an official.

Dave nodded, and then his smile faded as Thorne emerged from a cluster of suited men and women to stride towards him.

"Brace for impact," Dave muttered under his breath. "Excelsior," he said, with faux civility. "Good to see you this evening."

Thorne did not offer his hand, but drew himself up to Dave, leaning in and towering over him. His generous belly lurched towards Dave's chest, like an enthusiastic, badly-trained dog.

"You're going to see that Sandport is going to make the right choice tonight," he growled through a hot, breathy gush. "Don't think anybody fell for that fake news crap. Everybody knows what you are. Make sure your concession speech is good, Williams."

Dave shook his head and looked up directly into Thorne's eyes. "You always seem so angry. Maybe you should drink more herbal tea."

Thorne snickered. "Good, you'll need a sense of humour tonight. That'll see you through. My people are telling me it looks like we've clinched it. No surprises there, eh?"

He turned, slapped Dave's back with such force that Dave took an involuntary step forward, and was gone – striding back to his party staffers.

"Hey," said Amy, reappearing at Dave's side. "So, apparently they're about to declare. Any minute now. They'll come and get you, and then you need to get up on the stage with the returning officer for the result."

Dave looked at her. "Thorne said he thinks they've got it."

"I hear it's close," said Martha Lewandowski's voice, and Dave turned around to see her with Catie. For a moment, he thought they were holding hands.

"Oh, hi, Martha," smiled Dave. "Good to see you."

"You!" roared an American accent, and instinctively they turned to see Bart McClure stomping towards Martha.

"Oh, great," said Dave. "Anyone else from BEEF want to drop by and say hi?"

"Hello Bart," said Martha.

Bart drew himself up to her, cheeks flushed and wobbling with fury. Spittle leapt out of his mouth with enthusiasm. "What the hell kind of a piece was that, Lewandowski? Where's your independence?"

"It was a perfectly valid piece, Bart."

"I'll have your accreditation for this," he snarled, the curtains of his long, centre-parted hair quivering like a terrier. "Blatantly partisan!"

"Was it?" she replied. "I don't see why you're angry – surely the political suicide of the PM was an opportunity for you? Or are you just salivating at another delicious chance to shout at a woman? Now take a step back please, I can smell what you had for dinner."

Bart did step back, and he took a moment to survey the HHHP with the expression of a diner whose tiger prawns in garlic butter just twitched.

"You people," he said. "The dirty protest of British politics. Well, you're going to get wiped away tonight. Cleaned off."

Catie touched Martha's arm. "Come on," she said. "Let's not waste our time on this."

Bart pointed at Catie. "That little fella is right. Get out of here. Go and get your CVs ready for the job centre in the morning!"

An election official appeared at Dave's side.

"I'm sorry to interrupt," he said. "The returning officer is ready to make the declaration and asks that you join her on the stage. This way please, Mr Williams."

Dave looked at Amy, and she smiled back. "Whatever will be, will be," she said. The Happening Happy Hippy Party, and even Martha, all smiled in encouragement.

He nodded, and began the walk to the stage, making his way past journalists and camera crews speaking into headsets and cameras.

"Sandport's about to announce, ready with a live feed – estimate thirty seconds to declaration," barked a floor manager into her headset.

"You join us here in Sandport," a television journalist was explaining to a camera. "Traditionally one of the first constituencies to declare, tonight is no exception. It's been a dramatic election for this small town, seeing a high-stakes battle between BEEF's Excelsior Thorne and the HHHP's David Williams. And in just a few moments, we'll know what the people here decided."

And then, in what seemed like seconds, there Dave was. Standing in a semicircle of candidates on the stage, looking out at hundreds of people, and as many television cameras and microphones. He could hear the cheers and chants from the crowd outside the hall too.

The returning officer approached the sole microphone at the podium, cleared her throat, placed her glasses on her nose, and began.

☮

THE HAPPENING HAPPY HIPPY PARTY stood in the crowd, their eyes flitting between the returning officer and Dave. Catie felt Martha's hand slip into hers. She smiled.

"Declaration of results of poll," said the returning officer, reading from her papers. "I, the undersigned, being the returning officer at the election of a Member of Parliament for the Sandport constituency, do hereby give notice that the number of votes recorded for each candidate at the election was as follows. Richard Armitage, sixty votes."

"Who's he?" asked Rufus.

Dillon was squinting at his phone. "The 'Captain Sausage Fun-time and Complimentary Head Massage Party', apparently."

"Which one is he on the stage, then?"

"I suspect he's the one in the chicken costume."

Rufus shook his head. "These joke parties and their silly policies. Childish."

Catie and Dillon looked at him.

"Diana Geraldine Blythe. Five hundred and twenty votes," went on the returning officer.

"Okay, that's the Greens out," murmured Catie.

"Boris Fauntleroy-Pinkerton. Five thousand, nine hundred and four votes."

"There go the Conservatives," murmured Rufus. "They've definitely lost the seat."

"Janet Susan Neeson. Nine hundred and eighty-six votes."

"The Lib Dems are out," said Dillon.

"Kevin Gerald Smith. Two thousand, five hundred and sixty-seven votes."

"That's Labour," said Amy. "They haven't got it."

"Excelsior Ronaldo Thorne. Nineteen thousand, four hundred and eighty votes."

"Wow!" said Dillon.

"It's going to be tight," said Amy.

"David Basil Williams. Twenty-one thousand, five hundred and fifty-three votes. David Williams is duly elected as Member of Parliament for this constituency."

The crowd cheered. The other candidates applauded. Dillon punched the air. Catie danced. Amy whistled, and a tired but exhilarated smile spread across Dave Williams' face.

"His middle name's *Basil*?" said Rufus.

DAVE COULD NOT SEE Thorne's face as he stepped forward to give his victory speech, but Dillon would later describe it as bearing the expression of a pest control officer who came home to find his wife in bed with a giant cockroach.

Dave stepped forward and fished in his pocket for his speech. As he looked out at all the parties in the room applauding – with the exception of BEEF – he was reminded of the very first time he had spoken into a microphone like this. It was at Big Sue's Vegan Café, launching this campaign, a lifetime ago – and the lifetime of a completely different person.

If his smile were not already as broad as it could be, it would have lengthened by a few centimetres.

BART WALKED SMARTLY OUT of the community hall and into the car park, chatting into his phone. Alicia hurried to keep up.

"Bart! Where do you think you're going?" she demanded. "We've got damage limitation to do!"

"*Damage limitation*?" Bart laughed, ending his call and slipping the phone into his pocket. "What damage? This is mission accomplished, sweetheart. Break out the champagne."

Alicia caught up, and stepped in front of him, blocking his path.

"I don't know what you're talking about, but you need to get back in there and help deal with the media. This is only the start of the night – you're not sneaking away now that it's gone wrong."

Bart regarded her for a moment.

"Gone wrong? You've got no idea at all, have you, Medusa? It hasn't gone wrong. It's gone *right*. Very, very *right*."

He ostentatiously unpinned his black and red BEEF rosette, and held it up to her face. "See this?" he said. "It's not about this crap. It's about something so much bigger. This wasn't about getting Thorne elected. This was about having our vision normalised – rehabilitated – back into mainstream politics. And that, Cruella, is exactly what I've done."

Alicia was nearly speechless. "So, you don't care about BEEF's victory or defeat?"

"Are you kidding?" said Bart. "It doesn't matter a flying rat fart whether BEEF gets out of bed in the morning, never mind wins anything. Who cares about Excelsior Thorne? It's about whether BEEF's policies were picked up by the other parties. And you know what? They were. And *that* was the victory before a single vote was even cast. Influence, Alicia. Influence."

Bart let the rosette drop to the ground.

"Butterfingers," he shrugged, and resumed his brisk walk to the car.

Alicia stared at his retreating back for a moment, and resumed her follow.

"Do you really care about anything, then, Bart? Is it all just a game to you? Do you care about lives? About people?"

"I care about chaos, Cruella," said Bart as he clicked a keyfob, and the indicators of his Audi flashed in obliging response. "I want a new world order. We need a new world order. The only way to get that is war – social, and real. It's how to shake things up, rebuild whole chunks of civilisation. Read your history books."

"You're insane," she said. It was the only word that seemed able to filter through the fog of incredulity. "Insane."

He laughed. "Anyway, enjoy your pity party. I've got a long drive to London. I've accepted a new job."

"Where are you going?"

Bart opened the door of the car. "Director of communications for the – well, we'll see whether they're in opposition or government in the morning, right?"

He smirked, an inelegant grimace that would be Alicia's lasting impression of the man. With that, Bart Maclure ducked into the car and was gone, his damp rosette lying on the tarmac.

"Alicia! Alicia!"

She spun round. A junior party staffer was hurrying towards her. This one was Steve, with the pasty, anaemic complexion of so many of them. Steve's usual earnestness was in overdrive.

"Yes, Steve?"

"If you're here," he said, panting. "Who's looking after Thorne?"

Alicia's face fell. "Oh, *shit*," she said, and they hurried back into the hall where Thorne was standing alone with a large crowd of reporters and television cameras.

"So, I think that's the first thing we need to know, right? How did the Illuminati rig this election and on whose orders? There needs to be a full investigation. Was this ordered by the Pope? Is that who commissioned the operation to fill the ballot boxes with fake votes? I'm not saying it was – I'm saying we need to ask the question, and you can expect the lizard people to –"

Alicia stepped in front of Thorne, and cleared her throat. "What Mr Thorne means is that he has grave concerns about a number of issues relating to this election, which he may make further comment on in due course. Good night."

DAVE AND DILLON sat alone on a hill in the early hours of the morning, the orange lights of Sandport twinkling below them and beyond that, the big, black expanse of the English Channel.

There were journalists to speak to. Television broadcasts to participate in. Fizzy wine to drink. Speeches to give. It was a lot to do in one night, and Dave had slipped away with his closest friend for an hour or two of quiet. Up here in the cold May air, with phones on silent and nobody to interrupt, there was peace.

"Sandport is quite beautiful, you know," said Dave.

Dillon smiled. "What, from a distance? At night? Yes – that's probably about as beautiful as it's going to be."

Dave slipped out a hip flask, unscrewed the top and took a draught. "In those final moments, you know, I didn't think we had it."

"Well. You were right all along. Sandport *was* ready for a change. And it chose wisely."

Dave passed the flask to Dillon. "Just two thousand and seventy-three votes in it," he said.

"Thank you, South Coast Volkswagen Campervan Club," said Dillon, taking a swig. "I do like a Volkswagen owner."

"What now?"

"I guess you become an MP," shrugged Dillon. "You do, you know, MP things."

Dave nodded and sighed. "I suppose we should probably make a start," he said, pulling out his phone.

Sixty-eight missed calls, it informed him. Fifteen were from Amy.

He opened his mouth to say he'd better call her, and it rang again in his hand.

Amy, it said.

He answered. "Hi, Amy."

"Dave? Dave where the hell are you?"

"Just taking five with Dillon. You know, Sandport looks really beautiful from up here. Peaceful. I think –"

"What? Are you frigging high? You need to get back here right now!"

"Why? You're breathing funny. Is everything okay?"

Amy's voice sounded like it was only a few notches on the dial away from a scream. "How can you – do you not know, Dave? Dave how can you not know?"

Dave frowned. "Know what? What's happened?"

"We're winning, Dave!"

"Yes – I know, of course I know. I was there!"

"No, not the *seat,* Dave! The *election*! We're winning the general election!"

ACKNOWLEDGMENTS

This book has a long pre-history, and there are many people to thank as it took shape. I could not possibly list them all.

But I am deeply grateful to some who played particularly special roles in the journey of this story. So to Aidan Baron, Alex Blythe, Matt Fowler, Larissa Hansford, Chris Harrison, Denise Hunter, Sylvia Hunter, Emily F Jones, Denise May, Ryan Nicholson, Andy Reed and Carol Tsang de Campos - a very special thank you.

ABOUT THE AUTHOR

Alex Hunter is neither a hippy nor a politician. Although he did once meet a US Senator, and had a brief conversation in which it rapidly became clear that a word commonly used in British English for 'domestic cat' has a very different meaning in America.

Printed in Great Britain
by Amazon

41619551R00166